The Woodturner's FAQ Book

The Woodturner's FAQ Book

Frequently Asked Questions

Fred Holder

Linden Publishing

Fresno

The Woodturner's FAQ Book

by

Fred Holder

Cover design: James Goold

Book design: John Kelsey

357986421

ISBN 978-0-941936-94-1

Printed in Thailand

Library of Congress Cataloging-in-Publication data
Holder, Fred.
 The woodturner's FAQ book : frequently asked questions, with expert answers / by Fred Holder.
     p. cm.
 ISBN-13: 978-0-941936-94-1 (pbk. : alk. paper)
 1. Turning. 2. Woodwork. I. Title.
 TT202.H67 2007
 674'.8--dc22

                        2007006897

Linden Publishing Inc.
2006 S. Mary
Fresno, CA
www.lindenpub.com
800-345-4447

Table of Contents

FAQ

Introduction

This book was written as a result of the many questions that I have answered for beginning and intermediate woodturners over the last 10 years. This is not a how to turn book. Hopefully it will provide answers to the many questions that the reader has or will have as they begin the wonderful hobby of turning wood. The book has been divided into two parts: Part I addresses the question, "What do I need to turn wood?" and Part II addresses the question, "What do I turn?" Hopefully, I've answered most, if not all, of the questions that will come to mind as a person becomes interested in woodturning and finally takes the leap into this age old craft.

The book is organized into 12 chapters and the chapters are divided into a question and answer format. Some of this material is derived from questions that I have answered over the years. Some of it is from stories that I have written for my magazine, *More Woodturning*, and some

of it is new material to answer questions that I thought of as I was planning this book.

The book was designed to be a reference book that you take to your shop and when you encounter a problem, it will hopefully provide an answer. If you do not find the answer that you are seeking in this book, I invite you to send your question to me by e-mail (woodturner@fholder.com) and I will attempt to answer it or to find a source that will answer it for you.

Another source for asking and getting answers are the various newsgroups and message boards on the Internet. The one that I have read and responded to for many years is the newsgroup, rec.crafts.woodturning. I highly recommend it for almost any woodturning question.

--Fred Holder
March 2007

Part I—What do I need to turn wood?

FAQ **1**

Equipment for Woodturning

Figure 1-1. This stabilized boring bar set up has a laser pointer to gauge wall thickness in deep hollowing.

Q I want to start woodturning, what do I need?

As a bare minimum, you will need something to make the wood go around. This is generally done with a lathe. You will need accessories to help hold the wood onto the lathe and tools to use in carving the wood as it goes around. You will need some other shop equipment to prepare your wood for turning and to keep your tools sharp. Of course, you will need wood, and finally you will need some tools for finishing the project and a number of finishing solutions. Each of these will be discussed as this chapter progresses. Let us first look at the lathe.

Q What is a Lathe?

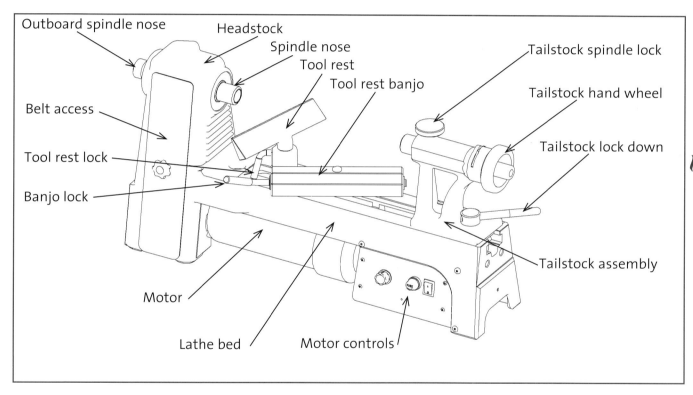

Figure 1-2. The basic lathe consists of a cast-iron bed, or ways, on which its various components are mounted.

The lathe is a device for holding wood and making the wood spin toward you so that you can apply a turning chisel to the wood and carve it to some desired shape. The basic lathe and its component parts are shown in the drawing of **Figure 1-2**.

The lathe consists of a metal bed mounted to a base or to a bench top. The bed has a milled top surface with a slot cut down the center to allow other parts to be mounted onto it. At the left end of the bed (as you face the lathe) is the drive mechanism or headstock. The headstock has a bearing-mounted shaft (called the spindle) on which is a multi-step pulley for driving the shaft from a power source. The spindle may have threads on each end, a hole through the center, and a female Morse taper recess in the right end.

(Note: A Morse taper is a designated standard taper for mounting rotating components that must run true. A complete Morse taper joint will consist of a female and a male part. When mated, they grip very well and run true.)

Most lathes have designations such as 1 inch x 8 tpi, which means the spindle diameter is 1 inch (25.4 mm) and the spindle has eight threads per inch. At the rear of the threaded area, there is generally a recess and then a machined shoulder, against which chucks and faceplates must register to run true.

At the right end of the bed is a moveable device called a tailstock. The tailstock will have a spindle that can move in and out for precision adjustment of the pointed center mounted in its Morse taper recess. The entire tailstock assembly can be moved back and forth on the bed to allow for shorter or longer pieces of wood to be mounted between the tailstock center and a drive center in the headstock spindle. When the position is very close, the tailstock assembly is locked to the bed and the final adjustment, of the tailstock spindle extension, is made to lock the wood between the two centers. Most tailstock assemblies can easily be removed when not turning between centers.

Another assembly is mounted to the bed between the headstock and the tailstock. This unit is called the tool rest assembly, consisting of the banjo, which is mounted to the lathe bed and can be locked in position. The banjo has a vertical hole to accept the post of the tool rest. The tool rest is generally a T-shaped piece and is adjustable above and below the center of rotation of the lathe spindle. This allows you to position the tool rest so that the tool achieves its best angle for cutting.

One final part of the lathe is the power unit. On the lathe in **Figure 2**, the power unit, a 1/2 horsepower direct current (DC) motor is mounted under the lathe bed. This motor is actually powered with 115-volt AC house current. The motor controller mounted on the front of the lathe bed makes the conversion to direct current and thus allows the motor to be variable speed. A step pulley is mounted on the spindle of the motor. The steps are reversed from those on the lathe headstock spindle. Moving the drive belt to a new step yields a different spindle rpm with the same motor rpm.

Q   What accessories will I need? What accessories will come with my lathe?

Basically, you can turn wood with just the accessories that come with a new lathe, that is, a faceplate, a drive center (for mounting in the headstock Morse taper), and a tail center (generally a live center these days) for mounting in the tailstock Morse taper. The faceplate is used to turn wood that is not supported by the tailstock. The two centers are used to hold and drive wood mounted between centers. **Figure 1-3** shows a sampling of these accessories.

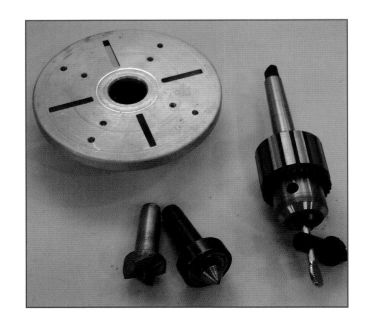

Figure 1-3. Here is a sampling of basic lathe accessories: top left is a faceplate, right is a Jacobs style chuck with a Morse taper to fit headstock and tailstock, center is a live tail center, and lower left is a spur drive center for the headstock.

Q Are there other accessories that I'll need?

Actually, for almost all woodturning, you do not need other accessories. The other accessories make the task easier or faster or are ways of compensating for vibration. The majority of these are tools to replace the faceplate and to make the mounting of wood easier and quicker. The four-jaw scroll chuck is the greatest invention for woodturners, see **Figure 1-4**.

The three-jaw scroll chuck has more limited uses and is mostly a hold-over from metal turning. It is for holding round stock, **Figure 1-5**.

After one has turned the outside and inside of a piece of wood (say a bowl), it is considered good practice to reverse the piece and final turn its base. There are many ways to do this, a four jaw scroll chuck with Cole jaws or jumbo jaws, a Longworth chuck (see **Figure 1-6**), or a vacuum chuck (See **Figure 1-7** and **Figure 1-8**). Of course, you don't need any of these, because the faceplate with a large piece of wood mounted on it could have a recess cut in its face to receive the top of the bowl. This latter assembly is called a jam-fit chuck. They have been around for many years, but are not as handy as the accessories mentioned here.

Finally, there are two types of steady rest available to help prevent vibration in the turning work. The center steady, **Figure 1-9**, is used for spindle work and is intended to prevent whip that can happen on long spindles. A recent addition to the list of accessories is the bowl-steady, **Figure 1-10**, made by Oneway Manufacturing in Canada. This steady helps support the thinning walls of the bowl as you hollow it out. As the bowl walls become thinner they flex and cause chatter as the cutting tool moves down the inside wall. The bowl-steady applies two bearing-mounted wheels to the outside surface of the bowl, to provide extra support directly opposite where the cutting tool is working. This stabilizes the turning and allows the turning of thinner walls with less skill.

Figure 1-4. This four-jaw scroll chuck has the wood worm-screw in place, making it a screw chuck.

Figure 1-5. The three jaw scroll chuck is very useful for turning wood.

Figure 1-6. The Longworth chuck holds a bowl for final turning of the foot.

Figure 1-7 A vacuum plate powered by a small vacuum cleaner holds a bowl for final turning of the foot.

Figure 1-8 This is a Oneway vacuum cup chuck for holding a bowl.

Figure 1-9. Center steady stabilizes spindles while turning.

Figure 1-10. This bowl steady, made by Oneway Manufacturing, stabilizes bowl walls while turning thin.

Q What turning tools will I need?

The turning tools that you will need depend upon the type of turning you will be doing. For example, it takes different tools to turn bowls than it does to turn spindles. It takes different tools to do things like hollow forms. There are several tool manufacturers that put out boxed sets of tools. I personally don't recommend purchasing a boxed set of tools. There are always tools in the box that you'll seldom use, you will accumulate enough of those over the years as your experience grows and you acquire more and more tools.

I have a set-up at the end of my lathe to hold five tools that I use regularly. These tools are shown in **Figures 1-11** and **1-12**):

1-inch (25mm) roughing gouge (**Figure 1-11**)

1/2-inch (12.5mm) spindle gouge (**Figure 1-11**)

3/16-inch (5mm) diamond parting tool (**Fig. 1-12**)

3/4-inch (20mm) skew chisel (**Figure 1-12**)

1/2-inch (12.5mm) skew chisel (**Figure 1-12**)

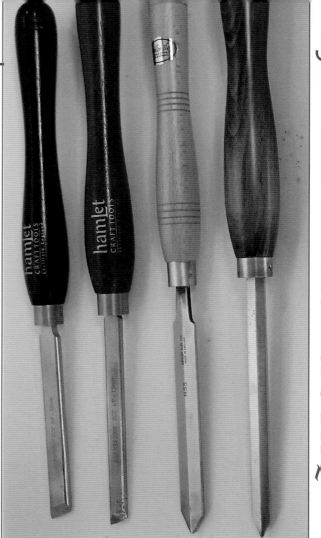

Figure 1-12. More spindle turning tools: 3/4-inch (20mm) skew chisel, 1/2-inch (12.5mm) skew chisel, two parting tools.

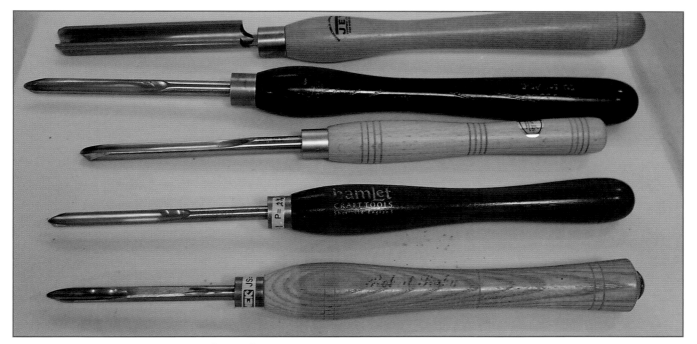

Figure 1-11. Here is a selection of spindle turning gouges.

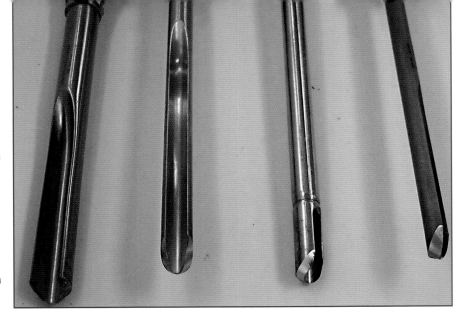

Figure 1-13. A selection of bowl gouges.

Figure 1-14. Robert Sorby round nose scraper (top) and Crown 1/2 inch (12.5mm) heavy duty round nose scraper (bottom).

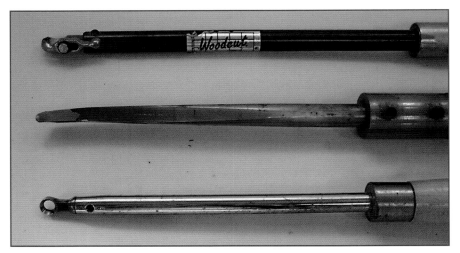

Figure 1-15. A selection of tools for hollowing end grain, top to bottom: Woodcut Pro-Forme hollowing tool, Kelton hollowing tool, and the Termite Ring tool from Oneway Manufacturing.

These tools are used mostly for spindle work. For bowl work, I add in my bowl gouges and scrapers, **Figures 1-13** and **1-14**. They are (left to right):

7/8-inch (22mm) bowl gouge from Robert Sorby (**Figure 1-13**)

5/8-inch (16mm) Crown bowl gouge with the Ellsworth grind (**Figure 1-13**)

5/8-inch (16mm) Henry Taylor bowl gouge with replaceable tip (**Figure 1-13**)

1/2-inch (12.5mm) Sweazey gouge with Ellsworth grind (**Figure 1-13**)

Large Robert Sorby half-round scraper (**Figure 1-14**)

Crown Tools 1/2-inch (12.5mm) heavy duty round-nose scraper (**Figure 1-14**)

Generally, hollow forms are turned with the grain running the length of the lathe bed or parallel to the axis of rotation. Therefore, most hollowing is done into end grain, which cuts somewhat differently than side grain. There are many tools that do this quite well, such as, the Oneway Termite ring tool, the Soren Berger tool, and a number of hollowing tools that are small-tip scrapers. Some of these tools are shown in **Figure 1-15**. Finally, for very deep hollowing, the stabilized rigs are very useful, especially those with a laser pointer to help determine wall thickness. See **Figure 1-1** on page 10.

Q What other shop equipment will I need?

You will need saws to prepare wood for turning and equipment to sharpen your turning tools. Where you get your wood will determine exactly what you'll need. Most woodturners use salvaged wood. This wood generally requires the use of a chain saw to cut it into usable sizes for mounting onto the lathe. A band saw is almost indispensable for the woodturning shop. I wouldn't want to be without one. No turning tool will hold its edge for very long, therefore, you will need a grinder. Woodturning tools do not have to be honed, but a grinder is essential.

Q Why do I need a band saw?

The band saw is the in-shop processor of wood. I don't know how I was ever able to be a woodturner without a band saw. You can cut pieces round on the band saw ready to mount onto the lathe. You can slice wood into thinner pieces to make laminates. You can use the band saw to remove parts of a turning to make it into something else. An example is the making of a little scoop. You turn a bowl like you will find on a goblet and then cut away a part of the bowl to convert it into a scoop. You could do this with a coping saw, but the band saw is much easier. The band saw is safer than the table saw, especially when working with wet wood.

Q Why do I need a chain saw?

A chain saw is necessary to convert logs and found wood into suitable sizes for turning. For years, I had a 16-inch (400mm) electric chain saw and a 12-inch (300mm) gas chain saw. The gas chain saw went into the woods to rescue downed timber or to where a tree had fallen and I had been invited to use some of it. This is when you want to offer a bowl to the owner of the tree in exchange for some of the wood. The electric saw was nice to use in the shop because there were no fumes. It was only as portable as my longest extension cord. I made these work for me for several years, but finally had to get a larger gas saw with an 18-inch (460mm) blade.

Q What do I need to sharpen my tools?

You can get as many recommendations on sharpening tools as there are woodturners. I learned to sharpen freehand over a long period of time and if I turned 8 hours a day 5 or 6 days a week, I would still freehand-sharpen everything. However, I don't turn more than 6 to 10 hours most weeks, and it is easier to use a sharpening jig to help retain the same profile each time. As my Christmas present to myself in 1999, I purchased a Woodcraft 8-inch (200mm) slow-speed grinder (1750 rpm) and the complete Wolverine sharpening system made by Oneway Manufacturing in Canada. This system performs very well for me.

One other grinding jig with which I am familiar is the Woodcut Tru-Grind tool sharpening system. I've had one of these for several years now and often use it for some tools. It is on a 6-inch (150mm) high speed grinder. It is less complex to use and has fewer parts than the Oneway system. Both systems produce good sharp tools with repeatable bevels. There are other sharpening jigs available, but I'm not familiar with them so will not address them here.

I should mention one other system that is quite useful, although a bit slow for woodturners: the slow-speed wet grinders such as the Tormek. You can get sharper tools from a Tormek than from any dry grinder. Unfortunately, they are slower to use and are considerably more costly.

If you can do nothing else, the purchase of a Veritas tool rest, and, if you don't have them already, the white aluminum oxide wheels, will significantly improve the grinding of your tools. I've never seen a grinder come from the factory with an adequate tool rest on it and few come with white aluminum oxide wheels.

Depending upon what you have in your shop, other things like a belt sander or even a disk sander can be used to sharpen your tools. If you don't want to spend the money right now on a grinder and jigs, there is another alternative. Make up a mandrel on a faceplate that will hold a grinding wheel. Then use your lathe as a grinder and hone your tools with a diamond hone in between grindings.

There is an article on my *More Woodturning* web site concerning sharpening. It doesn't deal with any of these fancy jigs. I do recommend a Veritas tool rest, which gives you a better base for holding your tool to the grinder. If you have Internet access, check out this web site on sharpening: www.fholder.com/Woodturning/article3.htm. Good luck, a sharp tool is one of the most important things you can have to make woodturning go right.

Q What wood will I need for turning?

Virtually any sound wood is suitable for turning. The harder woods generally turn cleaner and will hold details very well. The softer the wood, the sharper the chisel must be to cut it cleanly. Wood also cuts differently when mounted in the spindle mode (grain running parallel to the axis or rotation) and faceplate mode (grain running at 90 degrees to the axis of rotation). In the spindle mode you are cutting into side grain all of the way around the piece of wood. In the faceplate mode, you have side grain one-half of the time and end grain the other half of the time. This is, however, divided into two sections of side grain separated by two sections of end grain. For side grain you are cutting into the grain and it cuts much cleaner and easier. For end grain you are cutting across the ends of the wood fibers and it is much more difficult and much easier to tear out chunks of wood, leaving small pits in the surface.

You can visualize the fibers in a piece of wood by bundling together a handful of straws. The smaller the diameter of the straws, the stiffer the bundle. This is what happens as the wood becomes harder, its fibers are smaller and therefore closer together, making the wood dense and allowing it to hold greater detail. Appendix C lists a number of good turning woods along with their normal uses.

Figure 1-16. These commercial bowl blanks are ready to turn. They may be found simply cut into squares or cut round and sealed.

Q I'm going to turn spindles, what wood will be good for that?

Spindle-turning wood is generally cut into square sections of the length required for the job unless limited by the between centers distance of the lathe (**Figure 1-17**). These can easily be purchased in a wide range of woods. For architectural turning, such as newel posts and stair and fence spindles that will be painted, pine and fir are normal choices because of their reasonable cost and easy availability. If the turned pieces are not to be painted, but oiled or varnished, the choice becomes one of the harder woods, with oak often being the preference. The harder and more colorful woods are the choice of most furniture makers.

Note: When cutting on the surface of a spindle, "cut down hill," that is, from a high spot to a low spot. The reason for this is that you want the grain fibers that you are cutting to be supported by grain fibers below them. This allows the fibers to be cut as cleanly as possible. By cutting uphill, your chisel will tend to scoop under the ends of the grain fibers and lift them rather than cut them cleanly.

Figure 1-17. Wood used for spindle turning is generally cut into square sections.

Q What about woods for segmented turning?

Virtually any wood will work for segmented turning; however, if you mix woods, the woods should all have similar shrinkage characteristics. Different wood shrinkage rates place too much stress on the glue joints. I should also mention that the woods used for segmenting must be dry.

Any flat-sawn wood can be cut into segments for gluing up rings and finally for gluing up the total bowl blank ready for turning; **Figure 1-18** shows a segmented ring. One of the advantages of segmented turning is that the surface of the bowl being cut is all side grain. This makes it easy for a less skilled person to cut very clean surfaces.

Figure 1-18. This segmented ring has thin pieces of lighter wood inserted between each segment.

Q How do I finish my project?

There are many ways to finish your turning. You can reduce the amount of sanding required by cutting very cleanly with your turning tools. This means good sharp chisels and proper cutting techniques. It is best to finish the project when the wood is dry. Wet wood will generally warp as it dries, thus ruining or at best changing the beautiful shape that you had created. Also, wet wood tends to clog sandpaper quickly. Basically, however, finishing consists of making the surface of the project as smooth as possible and then applying some sort of sealing and protecting coat to help prevent the wood from drastically changing shape during changes in humidity. The normal way to make the wood smooth is by sanding.

Q What sort of tools do I need for sanding?

The sanding of a spindle is normally done with hand-held sandpaper. Sometimes a strip of sandpaper can be used to make a loop around the spinning wood. This is normally only done on a large area of the spindle where there are no decorations. The sandpaper must be used in sets of different grits. The coarse grit must be able to remove all of the tool marks left by the turning tools and any grain tear-out caused by improper cutting. Successively finer grits (as the grit become finer the number becomes larger) must be coarse enough to remove any scratches made by the previous grit. You can use steps like this: 80, 100, 120, 150, 180, 240, 320, 400, 600, 800. In some cases, you might start with 150 or 240-grit. This is often the case on spindles that were cut with a sharp skew chisel.

When sanding by hand, I recommend that you use a soft pad between your fingers and the sandpaper. This allows the sandpaper to more readily conform to the surface of the wood and keeps the heat generated by sanding away from your fingers. Many people use this method for sanding their bowls. Rotary sanders make easy work of bowl sanding. They come in two types: the self-powered rotary sander and the drill motor-powered rotary sander.

Q What is a self-powered rotary sander?

A self-powered rotary sander uses the friction between the surface of the rotating wood and the rotating tool to spin the sandpaper. This reduces the scratches often caused by hand sanding. **Figure 1-19** shows a self-powered rotary sander designed by Vic Wood of Australia. I'm not sure but I think Vic was responsible for inventing this sanding device. The 3-inch (75mm) wheel is fitted with a hook-and-loop material and the sandpaper is fitted with the loop material so that sanding disks can be quickly changed. On larger bowls, this is my favorite method of sanding. On smaller bowls, the disk is too large to rotate properly.

Figure 1-19. A self powered rotary sander designed by Vic Wood of Australia.

Q What is a drill motor-powered rotary sander?

A drill motor can be fitted with a Velcro disk holder (**Figure 1-20**). They generally come with a 1/8-inch (3mm) or 1/4-inch (6mm) shaft and a 1-inch (25mm), 2-inch (50mm), or 3-inch (75mm) padded surface fitted with the hook part of a Velcro mounting. The sanding disks are backed with the other half of the Velcro mounting. This tool has the advantage of its own power. This becomes very important when you have to stop the work to sand out a particularly bad rough spot. Normally, the lathe is run at some suitable speed (generally slower than you would use for cutting) and the sanding disk is applied on the far side of the bowl's interior for inside sanding and on the operator's side of the bowl for outside sanding. The drill can be a regular drill motor, one with a 90-degree angle, or one with a comfortable angle, like the Sioux sander shown in **Figure 1-21**.

Figure 1-20. A drill motor can power a rotary sander. Choose one that has a comfortable angle.

Q What should I use to seal or finish my turning?

It depends on the look you want. Some woods, such as cocobolo, are so oily that they only need to be sanded and buffed. Their own oil provides the shine. Most woods, however, require some sort of a sealer coat. This may be walnut oil (my favorite) or boiled linseed oil or a wax.

On porous woods, it is a good idea to apply a sealer coat before applying a finishing coat of lacquer or varnish. One such sealer is shellac, but there are several commercial mixtures such as Mylands Cellulose Sanding Sealer. All of these sealers need to be sanded back to the surface of the wood before applying any other finish. When using a spray-on lacquer, the sealer coat will keep the wood from absorbing more lacquer in one spot than in another, thus allowing for a better final finish.

If you are selling your work, you want it to shine, but you do not want it to look like plastic. High-gloss urethane lacquer will make your turning look like it is made from plastic. An old turner friend of mine, Wally Dickerman, says to put the shine on the wood before you apply the finish. Then it will not matter which finish you apply, since it is only going on as a sealer.

If you wish to buff the work, the Beall buffing system is a good choice. The Beall system uses three different cotton buffing wheels: one for Tripoli polishing compound, one for white diamond polishing compound, and one for carnauba wax. To use this system, you apply up to three coats of a drying oil on your turning. Watco Danish oil finish is a good choice. When this is dry, you then mount your buffing wheels onto the lathe spindle, run them at about 1800 rpm, apply the appropriate compound, and buff the surface smooth. When done properly, after the application of the carnauba wax polish, the turning will have a beautiful shine that enhances the beauty of the wood and does not leave it with a plastic look.

FAQ **2**

Choosing your Lathe

Figure 2-1. A foot powered lathe: this is a spring-pole lathe on demonstration at the joint AAW/ Utah Woodturning Symposium in the early 1990s at Provo, Utah.

Q Which lathe do I need?

The lathe that you will need depends upon what you plan to turn. If you simply want to turn some small spindles for a model that you are making and you own a drill press or even a hand drill, then mount the wood in the drill press chuck and rig up something to use as a tool rest. Some of my first woodturnings, after I reached adulthood, were little plugs for powder horns. I turned these in a drill press using the tang of a wood rasp ground at an angle for the turning tool. I later purchased a used Sears metal lathe. I could use this little lathe to turn those powder horn plugs much easier and I could use it to turn metal as well. It was very limited, but so were my needs at the time. I was shooting muzzle-loading rifles and doing blacksmithing as a craft, little woodturning was required and no special lathe was needed. From time to time, I needed to make a piece of wood round and put a little decoration on it. The small metal lathe met my needs. I'm saying this simply to illustrate that you do not have to have an expensive lathe to turn a small number of items of small size. Your hand drill clamped in a vise might do the job very well.

Most people making the decision to turn wood want something better than I've just described. In this chapter I hope to answer the questions that you will ask when trying to decide "Which lathe do I need?" I've also put together a number of tables that list new lathe models and some of their specifications. The specifications of most interest to woodturners are:

1. **Swing.** This is twice the distance between the center of rotation of the lathe and the bed of the lathe, that is, the maximum diameter of a piece of wood that can be mounted on the lathe spindle and rotated over the bed. This dimension is of greatest importance to the faceplate turner or bowl/platter turner, but is also important for the spindle turner who might turn large diameter spindles.

2. **Swing over the banjo.** This dimension is twice the distance from the center of rotation to the top of the banjo (the part that attaches to the lathe bed and holds the tool rest). This dimension is most important for spindle turners, since the banjo must be able to move freely under the rotating wood and all along the bed of the lathe. Unfortunately, it does not show up in lathe specifications very often.

3. **Distance between centers.** With centers mounted in the headstock spindle and in the tailstock spindle, this dimension is the length of wood that can be mounted between those centers for turning.

4. **Spindle diameter.** Another consideration must be how standard is the spindle nose diameter and its thread size. A non-standard spindle size can make it very difficult to get add-on accessories, such as chucks and faceplates.

5. **Morse taper.** It is nice to know which Morse taper the lathe has in both headstock and tailstock. A few of the older lathes had no Morse taper capability. They were very limited in use.

6. **Overall length** of the lathe or its footprint. This is important when deciding where the lathe can fit into your work area or shop.

7. **Whether it has indexing.** Indexing is not needed for most general turning. It does, however, become very important when you are adding decoration to a turning, such as equally spaced holes for different color wood inlays.

8. **Spindle lock.** Although not necessary, a spindle lock is a very handy thing to have when screwing on chucks and faceplates or removing them.

9. **Power.** How much horsepower does the lathe have and how do you vary the speed? Most lathes have three or more step pulleys on the lathe spindle and the motor shaft to allow some

variation in speed. Better lathes have motors that can be varied in speed, allowing you to better select the speed at which the wood turns smoothest.

In the tables I have divided the lathes into four groups:

1. **Small lathes.** Lathes that have 10 inches or less of swing and less than 24 inches (610mm) between centers are listed in **Table I**.

2. **Large lathes costing under $2000.** This group includes most of the hobby lathes. See **Table II**.

3. **Large lathes costing over $2000.** This group includes the heavy-duty production lathes and lathes for people doing larger work. See **Table III**.

4. **Lathes no longer available new.** This table lists some of the lathes that have gone off of the market in the last few years, but will still be available as used lathes from time to time. See **Table IV**.

In this chapter, I've divided my discussion

into four categories: spindle turning lathes, bowl turning lathes, mini-lathes, and foot powered lathes. The latter are not commercially available, but are something that you have to make yourself. Of course, you can also make a lathe yourself and many people have done this and will continue to do so in the future. I don't plan to tell you how to make your own lathe, but rather answer the questions that you may have concerning which lathe you should buy.

Most lathes that have a tailstock can be used for between-centers turning. Most lathes can also be used to turn bowls; however, there are some lathes specifically designed to turn bowls, which makes turning bowls easier because you stand directly in front of the rotating wood. The mini-lathes are a different category because they are designed to turn small items. They are therefore described in a separate section. Finally, I only include foot-powered lathes because they are a rich part of the woodturning heritage. If you should wish to turn wood and are participating in some historic event or re-enactment, a foot-powered lathe would be appropriate.

Table I. Small Lathes that have 10 inches (250mm) or less of swing, and less than 24 inches (600mm) between centers.

Mfr	Model	Swing	C-T-C	Swivel Head	Spindle	Morse Taper	Spindle Lock	Indexing	Power
Klein	Mini Lathe	5"	12"	No	3/4" x 16 tpi	No	No	No	No
Taig	Micro Lathe	4.5"	9.75"	No	3/4" x 16 tpi	No	No	No	No*
Sherline	4000/4100	3.5"	8"	No	3/4" x 16 tpi	No. 1/0	No	No	DC
Sherline	4400/4410	3.5"	17"	No	3/4" x 16 tpi	No. 1/0	No	No	DC
Jet	Pen Lathe	3.5"	8"	No	3/4" x 16 tpi	No. 0	No	No	60 W 0.05 A
Grizzly	G5967	6"	12"	No	3/4" x 16 tpi	No. 1	No	No	1/4 HP var
Vicmarc	VL 100	9"	14"	No	1" x 8 tpi	No. 2	Yes	24 pos.	No*
Jet	Mini	10"	14"	No	1" x 8 tpi	No. 2	No	No	1/2 HP
Jet	Mini var	10"	14"**	No	1" x 8 tpi	No. 2	No	No	1/2 HP var
Grizzly	G8690	6-1/4"	20"	No	3/4" x 10 tpi	No. 1	No	No	1/3 HP var
Oneway	1018	10"	18"	No	1" x 8 tpi	No. 2	Yes	24 pos.	No*
Delta	Midi	10"	14-1/2"**	No	1" x 8 tpi	No. 2	No	No	1/2 HPAC
Rikon	70-100	12"	16"	No	1" x 8 tpi	No. 2	Yes	12 pos.	1/2 HP AC

Notes:　* The lathe is available without power or there are optional power packages available.
　　　** Bed extension is available.

Figure 2-2. Sherline 4000

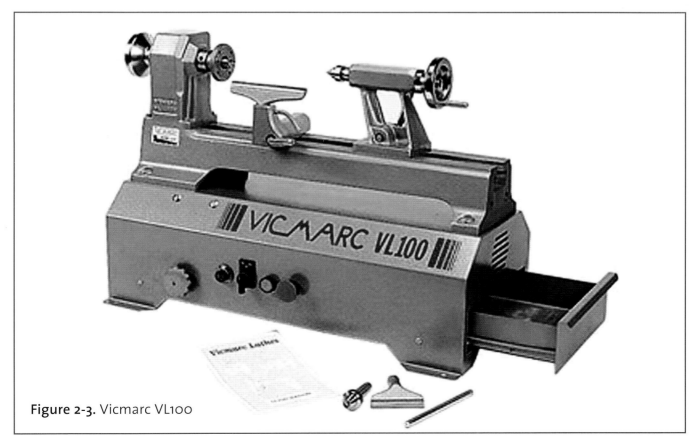

Figure 2-3. Vicmarc VL100

Table II. Lathes over 10" (250mm) swing and priced under $2000.

Mfr	Model	Swing	C-T-C	Swivel Head	Spindle	Morse Taper	Spindle Lock	Indexing	Power
Delta	46-715	14"	40"	No	1" x 8 tpi	No. 2	Yes	24 pos.	3/4 HP AC
Delta	46-745	16"	42"	No	1-1/4" x 8 tpi	No. 2	Yes	24 pos.	1-1/2 HP var
General	160	12"	38"	No	1" x 8 tpi	No. 2	?	?	3/4 hp
Grizzly	G8691	14"	40"	No	1" x 8 tpi	No. 2	No	No	1/2 HP AC
Grizzly	G1067Z	14"	40"	Yes	1" x 12 tpi	No. 2	Yes	24 pos.	1/2 HP AC
Grizzly	G1495	14"	40"	No	1" x 12 tpi	No. 2	Yes	12 pos.	1/2 HP AC
Jet	JWL-1236	12"	34-1/2"	Yes	1" x 8 tpi	No. 2	Yes	Yes	3/4 HP AC var
Jet	JWL-1442	14"	42"	Yes	1" x 8 tpi	No. 2	Yes	10 Pos.	1 HP AC var
NOVA	DVR 3000	16"	24"*	Yes	1-1/4" x 8 tpi	No. 2	Yes	24 pos.	1-3/4 HP var
Oneway	1224	12-1/2"	24"*	No	1" x 8 tpi	No. 2	Yes	24 pos.	1 HP var
VEGA	2400 BL	24"	17"	No	1-1/4" x 8 tpi	No. 2	?	No	**
Sears	Craftsman	15"	38"	Yes	1" x 8 tpi	No. 2	Yes	24 pos.	1 HP var

* Bed extensions are available
** Various options available or supplied without power unit

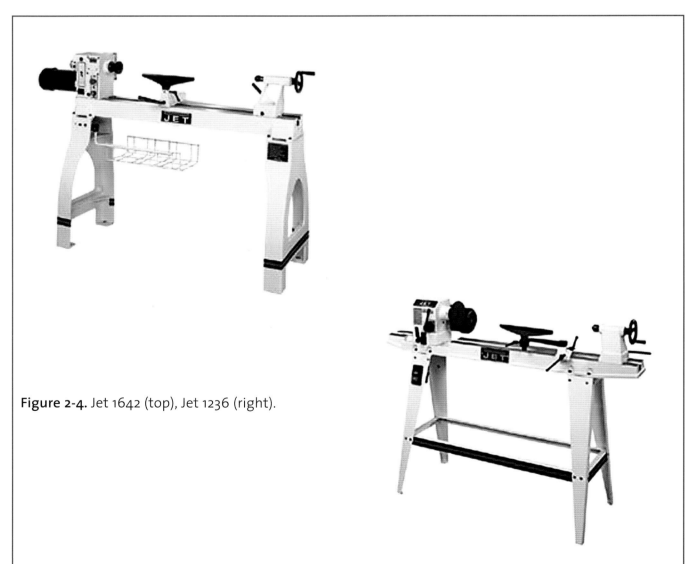

Figure 2-4. Jet 1642 (top), Jet 1236 (right).

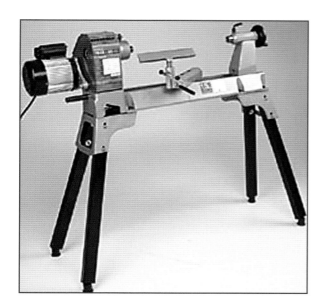

Figure 2-5. Nova 1624-44

Figure 2-6. Oneway 1224

Table III. Lathes over 10" (250mm) swing and priced over $2000.

Mfr	Model	Swing	C-T-C	Swivel Head	Spindle	Morse Taper	Spndl Lock	Index	Power
General	260	12"	38"	No	1-1/4" x 8 tpi	No. 2	Yes	Yes	1 HP var
General	26020	20"	38"	No	1-1/4" x 8 tpi	No. 2	Yes	Yes	2 HP var
General	25-600 M1	16"	43"	Yes/Slide	1-1/4" x 8 tpi	No. 2	Yes	36 Pos.	1-1/2 HP AC
General	25-650 M1	16"	43"	Yes/Slide	1-1/4" x 8 tpi	No. 2	Yes	36 Pos.	1-1/2 HP var
Oneway	1640	16"	40"	No	M33-3.5mm	No. 2/3	Yes	48 Pos.	Optional***
Oneway	2016	20"	16"	No	M33-3.5mm	No. 2/3	Yes	48 Pos.	1-1/2 HP var
Oneway	2416	24"	16"	No	M33-3.5mm	No. 2/3	Yes	48 Pos.	1-1/2 HP var
Oneway	2036	20"	36"	No	M33-3.5mm	No. 2/3	Yes	48 Pos.	1-1/2 HP var
Oneway	2436	24"	36"	No	M33-3.5mm	No. 2/3	Yes	48 Pos.	1-1/2 HP var
OmegaStubby	S500	11"/22"	16"/34"	No	1-1/4" x 8 tpi	No. 2	Yes	24 Pos.	1 HP var
OmegaStubby	S750	16"/30"	16"/34"	No	1-1/4" x 8 tpi	No. 2	Yes	24 Pos.	2 HP var
Powermatic	3520	20"	36"	No	1-1/4" x 8 tpi	No. 2	Yes	?	2 HP var
Robust	12x28	18"	28"	Slide	1-1/4" x 8 tpi	No. 2	Yes	48 Pos.	Optional
VEGA	2400 BTL	24"	17"	No	1-1/4" x 8 tpi	No. 2	?	No	**
Vicmarc	VL200 SB	16"	15"	No	1-1/4" x 8 tpi	No. 2	Yes	24 Pos.	**
Vicmarc	VL200 LB	16"	39"	No	1-1/4" x 8 tpi	No. 2	Yes	24 Pos.	**
Vicmarc	VL300 SB	24"	21"	No	1-1/4" x 8 tpi	No. 2	Yes	24 Pos.	**
Vicmarc	VL300 LB	24"	50"	No	1-1/4" x 8 tpi	No. 2	Yes	24 Pos.	**
VB Manuf.	VB-36 BTL	36"	Opt.	No	2-1/2" shaft	No. 3	Yes	No	Optional
Woodtek	96-130	20"	20"	No	1-1/2" x 8 tpi	No. 2	Yes	?	3 HP var
Woodtek	96-148	20"	38"	No	1-1/2" x 8 tpi	No. 2	Yes	?	3 HP var
Woodtek	96-248	20/36OB	20/18OB	No	1-1/2" x 8 tpi	No. 2	Yes	?	3 HP var
Woodtek	96-266	20/36OB	20/36OB	No	1-1/2" x 8 tpi	No. 2	Yes	?	3 HP var
Woodtek	96-3124	20/36OB	78"	No	1-1/2" x 8 tpi	No. 2	Yes	?	3 HP var
Nova	DVR-XP	16"	24"	Yes	1-1/4" x 8 tpi	No. 2	Yes	24 Pos.	1-3/4 HP var

* Bed extensions are available
** Various options available or supplied without power unit
*** Two Options available 1-1/2 HP and 2 HP 220 volt variable speed motors.

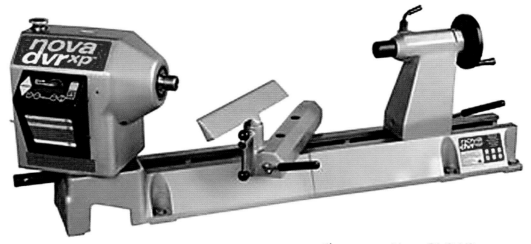

Figure 2-7. Nova DVR-XP

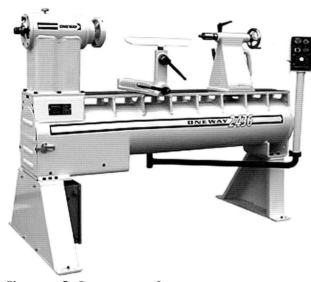

Figure 2-8. Oneway 2436

Figure 2-9. Vb 36

Figure 2-11. Vicmarc VL300 Shortbed

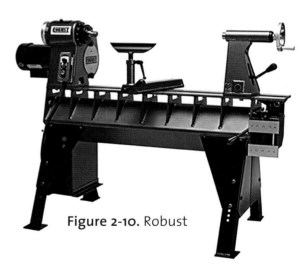

Figure 2-10. Robust

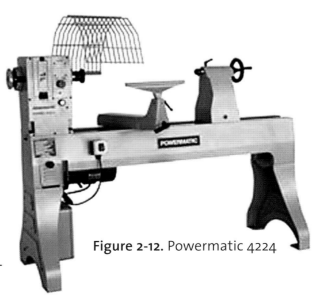

Figure 2-12. Powermatic 4224

Table IV. Lathes no longer commercially available

Mfr	Model	Swing	C-T-C	Swivel Head	Spindle	Morse Taper	Spindle Lock	Index	Power
Carba-Tec	3XL	6"	12.5"	No	3/4" x 16 tpi	No. 1	No	No	DC var
Nova	3000	16"	24"*	Yes	1-1/4" x 8 tpi	No. 2	Yes	24 pos.	**
Nova	Mercury	8"	8"	No	1" x 8 tpi	No. 2	No	No	? HP var
Nova	Comet	10"	14"*	No	1" x 8 tpi	No. 2	Yes	24 Pos.	**
Record	RPML	9"	12"	Yes	3/4" x 16 tpi	No. 1	No	No	1/3 HP AC
Record	CL-3-48	12"/20"	48"	Yes	3/4" x 16 tpi	No. 1	No	No	3/4 HP AC
Sorby	RS2F	13"/30"	24"	Yes	1" 8 tpi	No. 2	No	No	1 hp AC
Sorby	RS3F	13"/30"	36"	Yes	1" 8 tpi	No. 2	No	No	1 hp AC
Sorby	RS4F	13"/30"	48"	Yes	1" 8 tpi	No. 2	No	No	1 hp AC
Sorby	RS6F	13"/30"	72"	Yes	1" 8 tpi	No. 2	No	No	1 hp AC
Woodfast	M408-V	16"	16"	No	1-1/4" x 8 tpi	No. 2	Yes	24 Pos.	1-1/2 HP var
Woodfast	M908-V	16"	39"	No	1-1/4" x 8 tpi	No. 2	Yes	24 Pos.	1-1/2 HP var
Woodfast	M410-V	20"	16"	No	1-1/4" x 8 tpi	No. 2	Yes	24 Pos.	1-1/2 HP var
Woodfast	M910-V	20"	39"	No	1-1/4" x 8 tpi	No. 2	Yes	24 Pos.	1-1/2 HP var
Conover	——	16"	Var	No	1-1/2" x 8tpi	No. 3/2	?	No	***

* Bed extensions are available

** Various options available or supplied without power unit

*** The Conover Lathe was a kit package; components, power, and price depended upon options .

Q Which lathe do I need to turn spindles?

In spindle turning, the wood is mounted between two center points. One center point drives the work, known as the drive center.

The other, the tail center, is primarily a support point. How well these centers hold the work is important. If the wood moves on the center as it rotates, you will have problems and may get long spiral chatter marks on the surface. It is also a good idea to have drilled through headstock and tailstock spindles so that drill bits can pass through them for long-hole drilling. Any lathe with a tailstock and good bearings in the headstock can be used to turn spindles. Refer to **Tables** I through IV for suitable machines. As the size of the spindles increase, for example for pillars, a very sturdy and well-made lathe is needed. For normal furniture and stairway spindles, any lathe that has enough swing over the banjo and enough length between centers can handle these tasks. **Figure 2-13** shows a spindle turning lathe. If your work is long, you'll want one or more center steadies mounted on the lathe bed to reduce the tendency of the wood to vibrate, bow, or flex.

Figure 2-13. A spindle turning lathe holds the workpiece between centers.

Q What can I do to minimize movement on the drive center?

Most drive centers that come with new lathes have a center point and four chisel points to dig into the wood. With this type of drive center, the wood may move unless the center is firmly driven into the wood so that the four chisel points are buried in the end grain far enough to provide a firm support. With this type of center, you can make saw cuts on the end of the wood so that the chisel points are firmly embedded.

Another method that is very good, especially for beginning turners, is to use a dead cup-center designed for tailstock use as the drive center. This has a center pin and a cup with a sharp edge. The pin and cup dig into the end grain of the wood and provide enough grab to rotate the wood under normal turning pressure. A catch will stop the wood and perhaps prevent ruining the work. For many years I used one of these for all of my spindle turning, except very large pieces. Then a new drive center came on the market. It was designed for production turners who didn't want to stop the lathe between pieces, but it works great for turners who only turn occasionally. It is called the Steb center and is manufactured by Robert Sorby in England. The Steb center has a spring-loaded center pin and a cup with a number of sharp points around its rim. You can back off the tailstock and stop the spindle for inspection without stopping the lathe. You can also easily mount a spindle without stopping the lathe. When you are done inspecting the work, simply tighten the tailstock and the center is pushed into the Steb center and the sharp points again engage the work piece. A massive catch when driving the wood with a Steb center will cause the wood to rotate on the cup and save the workpiece.

Q Why would I want to drill holes in my spindles?

Turned wooden lamps need to have a hole up the center for the electrical wire to get from the base to the socket. I once turned a bunch of newel posts that had to be drilled up the center because they were to have lights mounted on their tops. There are a number of long-hole drills available to handle this job, but you must have drilled through spindles in both headstock and tailstock. Normally, when drilling long holes such as this, you want to drill from each end and have the two holes connect somewhere in the middle of the spindle. This ensures that your hole is on center at both bottom and top. If your stock is fabricated, you may have been able to leave a center hole when fabricating. If this is the case, try to have drive center and tail centers that will fit into the hole so that you are turning the wood with the center hole on the center of rotation. I have even used a long drill and a hand drill to drill long, deep holes through the wood before turning it. This requires that the centers support the wood on those holes. Some commercial tail centers with replaceable tips will have a special pin that can be slipped into the hole on the tailstock end. Sometimes a screw chuck can be used for a drive center.

Q What about a lathe for bowl turning?

Most lathes can be used for bowl turning. Some are designed specifically for bowl turning and may not have a tailstock. On these lathes you can stand directly in front of the lathe when hollowing your bowl. This is much easier than reaching over the bed of the lathe. The size of your lathe is completely determined by the size of bowl that you plan to turn. The swing of the lathe must be an inch or two more than the diameter of the finished bowl you plan to turn.

Some lathes are designed so that the operator may mount wood on the outboard end of the headstock and therefore have a bowl lathe. Oneway Manufacturing has outboard tool rests that can be used for outboard turning. You can also use a free-standing tool rest when turning outboard. Other brands have a sliding headstock that can be slid down to near the end of the bed for bowl turning. Others use a swiveling headstock, which allows you to rotate the headstock outboard for turning bowls. This considerably increases the swing of the lathe. The NOVA DVR 3000 lathe is one such. It has a 16 inch (400mm) swing over the bed, but with an outboard turning attachment it can swing almost 30 inches (760mm). I don't have the outboard turning attachment, but I can rotate the headstock out to the first indent (about 30 degrees) and still use the normal tool rest on the lathe to hollow bowls. I have also rotated the headstock to the back of the bed and mounted slightly oversize stock for turning down until it would swing over the bed of the lathe.

Q What is a mini-lathe?

I have defined a mini-lathe to be one with a swing of 10 inch (250mm) or less and a center-to-center distance of less than 24 (600mm) inches. These lathes are listed in Table I. The mini-lathes first came on the market in the late 1980s or the early 1990s. The first of them that I encountered was at the joint American Association of Woodturners/Utah Woodturning Symposium at Brigham Young University, Provo, Utah in 1992. There was a Klein Design Lathe and a Carba-Tec lathe. Both lathes had 3/4 inch by 16 tpi thread sizes on their headstock spindles. The Klein Design Lathe does not have Morse taper capabilities in either headstock or tailstock. The Carba-Tec was a little larger; the Carba-Tec specifications are listed in Table IV. Neither of these lathes came with their own power supply. A short time later, a mini-lathe from Vicmarc in Australia came on the market. The Vicmarc VL-100 had a 10 inch (250mm) swing and 14 inches (350mm) between centers. The Jet is one of the most popular mini-lathes. It has flooded the market with its reasonable price and easy availability.

The largest lathe that I've included in the mini-lathe category is the Oneway. It is the most capable of the small lathes. These lathes have all of the functions of the larger lathes, they just limit the size of the turnings that can be produced. The Vicmarc and the Oneway lathes are well machined and precise in their operation.

Q What is a foot-powered lathe?

Originally, all lathes were foot powered. Initially, a spring-pole lathe was the primary lathe of choice for many woodturners. The bodgers of England went into the woods, cut down trees, built a shed with a spring-pole lathe inside, and began turning chair spindles right on site. This was done until just before the Second World War. The spring-pole lathe had a method of placing the wood to be turned between centers. A springy pole was then mounted above the lathe. A rope or thong was attached to the springy pole and brought down and a wrap or two was taken about the spindle to be turned. The thong continued on down to a foot pedal. When the operator depressed the foot pedal, the thong was pulled down, thus rotating the workpiece. The workpiece rotated toward the operator on the downward stroke and he could cut the wood. When he released the foot pedal, the springy pole pulled up on the thong and rotated the workpiece in the opposite direction. During that part of the cycle, the tool was pulled away from the wood. This was the simplest of lathes and was used for many years. **Figure 2-1** on page 22 shows a spring-pole lathe.

The next development was the treadle lathe, which worked much like a treadle sewing machine. This lathe had a spindle and a large flywheel that helped even out the rotation. The operator worked the treadle of the machine with his foot, adding power to the flywheel. A flat belt from the flywheel drove the lathe spindle. This lathe worked much like the modern-day lathe except for the method of powering the spindle.

When I retired in 1993, I planned to supplement my retirement income by selling woodturnings at craft shows. Since many craft shows did not have power available and I thought a demonstration would help pull people in to my booth, I built a modified spring-pole lathe. I didn't use a springy pole, I used a bungee cord instead. I called this a modified spring-pole lathe because it also had a spindle and would accept chucks and faceplates and different drive centers. The thong was attached to the bungee cord, wrapped a couple of times around the spindle, and then passed down to a foot pedal. I got a full three revolutions forward for turning and became very good with this little lathe. The side benefit was that I significantly gained tool control through the use of this lathe.

Q So how do I decide what lathe to buy?

As you can see, a lathe is a device to hold the wood and make it go around while you carve it with a chisel. You simply have to decide what sort of objects you plan to turn, how large they are, and how much money you want to spend. I have not told you which lathes I think are best, but I have given you some idea of what is available. Any of the lathes that cost close to $2000 and up are very good performers and suitable for a person trying to make a living from turning. Lathes costing less than $2000 fall into the hobby class. The more you pay for your lathe the more you can expect from it. Remember, however, the price of the lathe is only the beginning of the expenses. You have to have lathe and shop accessories, turning tools, and wood. The accessories and turning tools may considerably exceed the price of the lathe over time.

FAQ 3

Turning Tools

Figure 3-1. Stuart Mortimer uses a rotary rasp to refine a hand-made spiral at the 2005 Utah Woodturning Symposium.

Q Which turning tools do I need?

There are three types of turning tools: the gouge, the skew chisel, and the scraper. Exactly what tool mix you will need depends upon the type of work you will be doing. Each of these tools has specific functions.

Q What is a gouge?

A gouge has a U shaped cross section. In the early days, they were all forged out of flat tool-steel stock. Some of the gouges had very shallow flutes, that is, their cross section was similar to the very bottom of the U. These were generally used for detailed work in spindle turning. The roughing out gouges had a more complete U shape and were ground straight across on the end. Today, most of the roughing-out gouges are still forged from flat stock. However, most spindle gouges are milled from round stock, that is, a flute is milled in the round bar. These flutes are generally deeper than they were in the forged version. Finally, there is the bowl gouge, which is made from solid round stock with a deep flute milled in it. Tools made from round stock are generally quite strong because the tool is the same diameter all of the way into the handle. On the forged tools, there was generally a forged tang that was smaller in diameter than the rest of the tool. All of these tools have a bevel, or cutting edge, ground on the very end of the flute.

Q What is a skew chisel?

The basic skew chisel design is made from a rectangular cross section of tool steel and has its cutting end ground at an angle of about 70 degrees, as shown in **Figure 4-2** on page 43. The cutting edge has a bevel on each side of the tool that brings the actual cutting edge to the exact center of the stock. Angles of 25 to 45 degrees are recommended for this tool. The 25 degree tool cuts very well, but requires much skill to use. A friendlier grind angle is 40 to 45 degrees and is necessary on very hard woods. Originally, skew chisels had sharp square edges that would dig into your tool rest and make nasty marks in the surface of the tool rest. Today there are alternatives: skews with the corners ground off, oval skews, and round skews. The long point of the skew cutting edge is the one that extends the furthest. The short point, or heel, of the skew is the other point of the cutting edge. This tool planes the wood very smooth. It can be used to cut excellent V grooves into the surface, it can be used to clean up flat surfaces cutting across the end grain, it turns beautiful beads, and if you are not careful it will turn unplanned "decorative" spirals down your nearly finished turning. It is one of the most useful spindle turning tools, but it does not do small coves well.

Q What is a scraper?

A scraper is a rectangular piece of tool steel that has a cutting edge with an 80 to 90 degree bevel. The tool is used with the cutting edge at near center line, but with the end of the handle higher than the cutting edge. On softer woods, the part that cuts the wood on this tool is a little burr that turns up on the top of the tool when it is sharpened. This burr is small and fragile and must be replaced often with regrinding or with some sort of burnishing tool that will roll up a new burr. The cutting edge of scrapers takes many shapes from square across to coves in the tip to allow the cutting of beads. Many people make up scrapers and grind them to shape to produce a particular pattern. The tool cuts by simply being shoved into the wood. On softer woods, the scraper will often tear out chunks of grain. When used on very hard woods, it is necessary to remove the burr from the tool and simply cut with the very edge of the tool. It may also require a bit more bevel angle, say 70 degrees, to cut well. Any tool that does not have a sharp cutting edge will be designated as a scraper. A recent addition to the scraper family is the hardwood scraper from Robert Sorby, which has a bevel on the top of the tool as well and the normal bevel. This tool is used with the bevel rubbing on the wood. To use on softer woods, it needs to have a burr generated by grinding a normal bevel.

Q What do I need for spindle turning?

A roughing-out gouge, a detailed spindle gouge, a skew chisel, and a parting tool will be needed for spindle work. These tools are shown in **Figure 3-2**. The roughing out gouge is used primarily for making the wood round, but because of its long sides it can perform many of the smoothing functions of the skew chisel. The roughing gouge that is most common is a one-inch diameter tool, that is, one inch across the cross section of the U shape. These are also made larger, up to two inches across. This tool is generally ground straight across the end and with a bevel angle of 40 to 45 degrees. The polished flute channels the shavings away from the cutting edge. The tool is used to rough the wood mounted between centers to round. It is

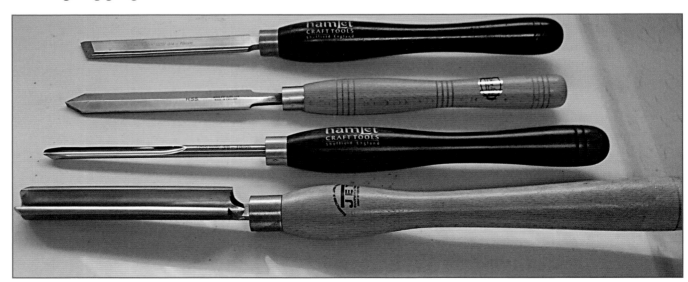

Figure 3-2. Spindle turning tools (top to bottom): Skew chisel, parting tool, detail spindle gouge, and roughing gouge.

not recommended for making cuts on a piece of wood running with the grain perpendicular to the axis of rotation or in bowl mode. There are two reasons for this. First, because it is ground straight across it is easy to catch one of the corners when hollowing a bowl, and second, because the tang is the weakest part of the tool and it is subject to breaking with a massive catch. A skillful turner using this tool can make a very smooth surface on a spindle.

The detail gouge, or spindle gouge, has a shallow flute and serves to put in the details on a spindle turning. The cutting end is ground into a fingernail shape. A 20 to 30 degree grind angle is most useful on a detail spindle gouge. The smaller the angle of grind, the sharper the edge will be; however, it will also be more fragile and require greater skill to use. I normally use about a 30 degree angle on my detail spindle gouges and find this suitable for most spindle turning tasks. The detail spindle gouge is used to make beads and coves on the turned spindle. It can also be used on the outside of small bowls. However, with a 30 degree grind angle it is not suitable for the hollowing of a bowl, other than in the very early stages of hollowing. A fingernail grind, especially if the wings of the gouge are ground back considerably, works very well to hollow end-grain items such as goblets and little boxes. In cutting end grain the cuts should all be made from center toward the outside edge.

The skew chisel is used both to plane the surface smooth and straight and to do some of the detail work. The skew chisel is sharpened with a double chamfer and a skewed edge. This is the only tool that I recommend honing after grinding. Note that when you look at the edge, if you can see it, the tool is not yet sharp.

The parting tool is like a skew chisel except that its edge is straight across. It is narrow, 1/16 inch (1.6mm) to 1/4 inch (6mm), and deep. It is used to part off the turning and to make deep sizing cuts. When really fine detail is required, the parting tool can function like a skew chisel.

Q I expect to be doing faceplate work (bowls) what will I need?

The tools illustrated in **Figure 3-3** will handle most faceplate and bowl work. You will need one or more bowl gouges and one or more heavy-duty scrapers to handle most of the faceplate or bowl work. For outside work, the scrapers need to be straight edged. On the inside of the bowl, round nose or half-round scrapers serve very well.

The bowl gouge is a much longer tool than those designed for spindle work. They have a longer and deeper flute and longer handles. The flute shape varies from manufacturer to manufacturer. Many are the conventional U shape, but not as much so as a roughing gouge, and they range in shape to almost a V shape in the most radical designs. A great many bowl gouges will come from the factory with a straight-across grind, like the roughing gouge. Many turners use the straight-across

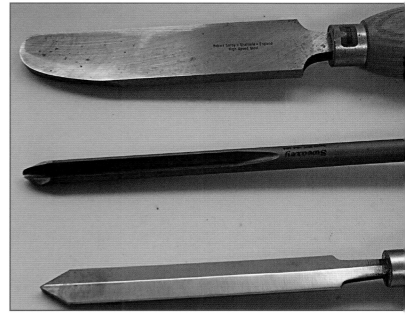

Figure 3-3. Faceplate turning tools (top to bottom): round nose scraper, bowl gouge, and parting tool.

grind. However, when used on the inside of the bowl, the straight-across grind can easily cause massive catches in the hands of an inexperienced turner.

The bevel angle on bowl gouges range from about 40 degrees to 65 degrees. A 40 to 45 degree angle works best for the first part of the hollowing of a bowl and will work fine for a shallow bowl or plate. As the hollowing becomes deeper, the tool shaft will come against the edge of the bowl and will prevent you from rubbing the bevel on the wood, and the cutting will become difficult. Many turners have a second bowl gouge ground with a bevel angle of 60 to 70 degrees that they can use to finish-turn the inside of the bowl. David Ellsworth, a well-known United States woodturner, developed a grind that has swept

back wings and a nose bevel angle of about 65 degrees. Crown Tools manufactures this gouge to David's specifications. This one tool can turn down the inside of a bowl and on across the bottom in a single pass.

I don't recommend that you use either the skew chisel or the roughing-out gouge on faceplate work. Unlike spindle-turned work where the grain is the same all of the way around the workpiece, faceplate work has a change in grain direction four times each revolution. This can make for massive catches with the skew chisel and can often put so much stress on a roughing-out gouge that the tang breaks where it enters the handle. A detail gouge may perform well on the outside of the bowl when making fine finishing cuts or cutting in beads and coves.

Q What will I need for eccentric work (multi-centered turning)?

A spindle gouge, of about 3/8 inch (10mm) cross section, or a 3/8 inch (10mm) bowl gouge, will do most of the work for multi-center turning. I do not recommend the use of a skew chisel or scrapers on multi-center work. Neither work

well when the tool is only cutting during a part of a revolution. You can do multi-centered work between centers or with one of the many chucks on the market. In all cases, use a gouge to cut this multi-center work.

Q What chucks are available for multi-center turning?

Figure 3-4. Escoulen ball and socket chuck, Sorby eccentric chuck, Axminster eccentric chuck (bottom).

Three chucks available in the United States are shown in **Figure 3-4**: the Robert Sorby eccentric chuck, the Escoulen ball and socket chuck, and the Axminster eccentric chuck. Each of these perform a slightly different function and have their place in multi-center turning. The Robert Sorby chuck shifts the center of rotation of the mounted wood up to about 1-1/2inch (38mm). The Escoulen chuck tilts the wood in the chuck and allows for different types of eccentric shapes. The Axminster eccentric chuck shifts the center of rotation in steps. This is the only chuck that can return to a previous position exactly. Each of these have their place in the turning shop.

Q How can I do multi-center work between centers?

The wood must be considerably larger than the finished piece of eccentric work. Prior to starting, the end of the wood is laid out similar to **Figure 3-5**. The wood is then turned round between centers, but leaving one inch or so of the wood square on each end. After it is round, the centers are shifted to one of the offset points and a part of the spindle is turned to some shape. The center points are again shifted and more turning is done. One cannot do as many things between-centers as can be done with the eccentric chucks.

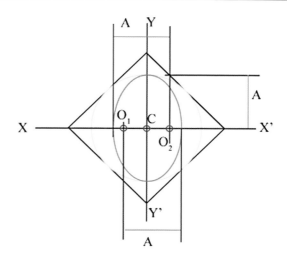

Figure 3-5. Layout of end pieces for multi-center turning.

Q I plan to hollow some vases, what will I need?

There are two types of hollowing tools used for deep hollowing: scraping tools and cutting tools. Most of the hollowing tools on the market are scrapers, but there are a few that use a ring type tool with a limiting cover. The limiting cover allows you to set the depth of cut and makes the tool easier to use. Normally, these tools are mounted in a long handle to give the operator more leverage. As the hollowing goes deeper, the overhang across the tool rest becomes very difficult to handle. Enter the stabilized hollowing system, which uses two tool rests to remove the stress from the operator.

Q What do these hollowing tools look like?

Figure 3-6 shows a number of hollowing tools that are on the market. These tools are normally fitted into a long handle to help the operator to resist the pressure of tool overhang. The cutting tip of these tools is small to reduce the torque created by the tool cutting the wood.

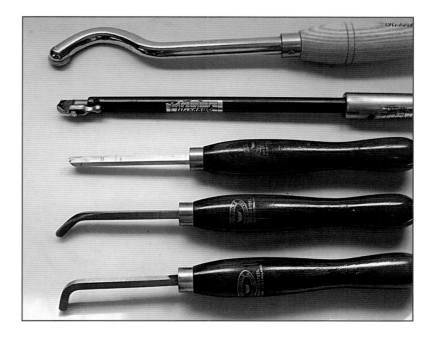

Figure 3-6. A selection of hollowing tools (top to bottom): Robert Sorby multi-tip hollowing tool, Woodcut Pro-Form hollowing tool, and bottom three are a set of small hollowing tools from Crown Tools.

Q What about the stabilized hollowing systems?

Figure 3-7 shows a stabilized hollowing system with a laser pointer attachment that helps judge the wall thickness of the turning. The handle is quite a bit longer than a normal handle and, in addition, the system has a secondary tool rest that also prevents the tool from rotating. The stabilized hollowing systems remove the operator stress from the operation. The laser pointer, which is set some distance from the cutting tip, helps the operator to judge the wall thickness of the hollow form.

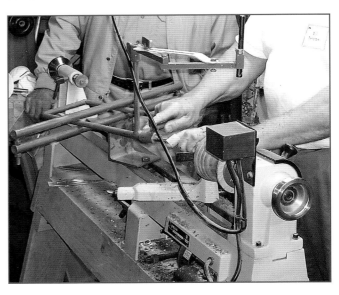

Figure 3-7. This home-made stabilized boring bar and laser pointer setup is being used to hollow a small vase.

Q I want to turn little boxes, what tools will I need?

Figure 3-8. Small wooden box with lid removed.

To turn little boxes like the one shown in **Figure 3-8**, you will need a spindle gouge and a square-end scraper. Actually, I prefer the box tool made by Crown Tools, which is made from 3/8-inch (10mm) round stock. The top is ground down almost half-way through and a bevel of about 80 degrees is ground on the end. This tool is not ground straight across, but is canted a few degrees so that you can cut down the side of the box and into the corner without the other edge of the bevel cutting the bottom of the box.

Q I want to make some spiral flutes on my turnings, what tools will I need?

Normally, the woodturner lays out the spiral on his turned workpiece and then uses a saw, chisel, and a round rasp to cut the individual flutes by hand. **Figure 3-1** on page 34 shows a hollow form that has spiral openings cut in its side. I would also recommend Stuart Mortimer's book, *Techniques of Spiral Work*.

Q I want to make some threads in wood, what tools will I need?

There are several ways to make threads in wood, all of which are described in my book, *Making Screw Threads in Wood*. The two most commonly used methods by woodturners are hand thread chasing, and the use of a threading jig on the lathe. Hand thread chasing has been done for centuries and once mastered is the preferred method.

Q What tools will I need to do hand thread chasing?

The basic tools needed for hand thread chasing are shown in **Figure 3-9**. The normal thread chasers are sold as a set, one for the inside and one for the outside threads. A woodturner that watched one of my demonstrations didn't want to spend the money for the tool. He came up with a new tool made from a bolt. His name is Bruce Campbell of British Columbia, Canada. It works quite well and is inexpensive to make. Bruce's tool puts both the inside chaser and the outside chaser into one tool. Using these tools does require considerable practice. One must develop a rhythm to ensure that an even thread is cut. Allan Batty from England has made up a very good video, *The Definitive Work on Hand Thread Chasing*. Also see *All Screwed Up*, a book by John Berkeley.

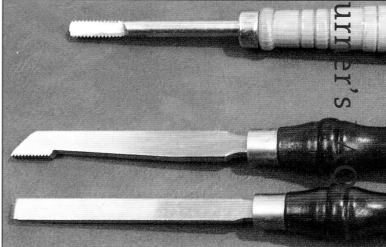

Figure 3-9. Hand thread chasers: a homemade thread chaser made from a 3/8-inch (10mm) bolt, top, provides for both inside and outside chasing.

Q What about the threading jig?

The threading jig shown in **Figure 3-10** was designed by Bonnie Klein and is currently available with adapters for several lathes. It is possible to make up adapters for using this jig on virtually any lathe. With this system, you need a lathe and the threading jig. The threading jig holds your chuck or faceplate with the mounted wood to be threaded. It then moves the wood forward into a rotating cutter mounted in the headstock spindle. As the wood is moved forward toward the cutter, it is rotated at a set rate of threads per inch. The cutter cuts a thread in the rotating wood. This is a simple system to use and easier to learn than hand thread chasing.

Figure 3-10. The Bonnie Klein threading jig can be adapted to fit any lathe.

FAQ 4

Sharpening

Figure 4-1. For best results, use a white aluminum oxide grinding wheel, because it runs cooler and stays sharp better than the grey kind of wheel. Once the bevel has been established, set the tool rest to maintain the bevel and roll the tool to grind it evenly.

Q What is needed to sharpen my turning tools?

Many woodworking tools are sharpened on a bench stone and only ground to get the initial shape. This technique does not work as well when sharpening woodturning tools, partially because the edge of the tool is often removed in a matter of seconds when the tool is pushed into the wood. A grinding device of some sort is required to sharpen woodturning tools. This may be a bench grinder, a sanding disk, a belt sander, or a grinding wheel mounted on your lathe. I prefer a bench grinder with white aluminum oxide wheels, **Figure 4-1**. For people who do not turn every day, I also recommend grinding jigs to help in making repeatable bevels and shapes. Regardless of which grinding device you are using, each of the tools (skew chisel, gouge, and scraper) requires a different treatment when sharpening. Note that when you look straight at the edge of a skew chisel or gouge, if you can see it, the tool is not yet sharp.

Q How do I sharpen my skew chisel?

The skew chisel is sharpened with a double bevel and a skewed (slanted) edge (**Figure 4-2**). This chisel is often used for turning flat surfaces. The chisel is conveniently sharpened with the wide part of its shaft laying flat on the tool rest. The angle of the grinder tool rest is set so that the bevel of the tool would mate with the surface of the grinding wheel. The skewed edge must be straight across (horizontal) the surface of the grinding wheel (**Figure 4-3**). The tool bevel is then moved back and forth across the grinding wheel until the wheel is grinding clean all of the way to the edge of the tool. The tool is then flipped over and the same operation is repeated for the other bevel. When completed, the cutting edge should be located central to the tool shaft.

This is the only tool that I recommend honing after grinding.

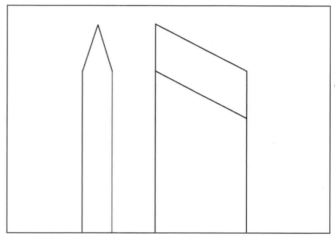

Figure 4-2. This drawing shows the configuration of the edge of the skew chisel.

Figure 4-3. To grind the skew chisel, move it back and forth across the tool rest with the cutting edge horizontal.

Q How do I sharpen my gouges?

Figure 4-4. Set the tool rest so that the bevel of the tool is against the grinding wheel.

Figure 4-5. A square-across tool, such as a roughing gouge, is ground by rotating the tool on the tool rest.

Figure 4-6. Grind a spindle gouge with swept-back wings by moving the tool up the grinding wheel.

All gouges, except the roughing gouges, work best with a fingernail grind on their end. I find they work better if the wings of the gouge are also swept back. This gives you a longer cutting edge and more options for cutting. This is done by setting the grinder tool rest so that the bevel of the gouge would mate with the surface of the grinding wheel (**Figure 4-4**). The gouge is then rotated from left to right in a straight across grind, such as is required for a roughing gouge (**Figure 4-5**). For a fingernail grind, the tool is rotated to the right and the tool is slid up the wheel as it is rotated. This is done on both sides until the desired shape is achieved (**Figure 4-6**). This is difficult to learn and that is why grinding jigs are so important, especially for beginning turners. The only honing I recommend on gouges is the inside of the flute with a small round tapered stone. This removes the burr and makes the tool cut longer.

Q Tell me about the standard grinder with white wheels?

Any standard grinder will work to grind your turning tools. Standard grinders are either 6 inch (150mm) or 8 inch (200mm) wheels and either high speed (about 3700 rpm) or slow speed (about 1750 rpm). They come with grey wheels for normal grinding duty. White aluminum oxide wheels are recommended for sharpening woodturning tools. They are more friable and are less liable to clog with bits of metal. Any wheel must be dressed regularly to keep it sharp. A sharp grinding wheel will remove more metal with less heat. When your tool starts to overheat it is likely time to resurface your grinding wheel. A grinding jig will be very helpful in obtaining sharp tools with a consistent grind. Two jigs that will work well with a standard grinder are the Oneway Wolverine grinding jig made in Canada and the Tru-Grind tool sharpening system made in New Zealand. Either of these will do a good job of grinding tools without much skill. If you want super sharp tools, the Tormek sharpening system is a good choice, but you still need a standard grinder for the rough shaping of tools.

Q How do I sharpen scrapers?

The scrapers are sharpened with their shaft flat on the rest of the grinder. Set the angle of the rest so the bevel of the tool will mate with the surface of the grinding wheel (**Figures 4-7 and 4-8**). Then move the tool back and forth across the rest or rotate it as necessary to keep the edge in contact with the wheel. When the entire bevel right up to the edge has been ground clean, there should be a small rolled burr along the top of the cutting edge. For softer woods, this burr is the cutting edge and should not be removed. For harder woods, the burr should be removed with a stone. The grinding bevel for scrapers is shown in **Figures 4-9** and **4-10**.

Figure 4-8. This is how to position a scraper for grinding its bevel.

Figure 4-7. This scraper is being sharpened on the Tormek system.

Figure 4-9. Here is the end view of a correctly sharpened scraper. The edge falls away at about 10 degrees from vertical.

Figure 4-10. Here is the side view of the correctly ground scraper. .

Q What is a Oneway Wolverine grinding jig?

In December 1999, I bought a new slow-speed grinder and a Wolverine grinding jig. It significantly improved my tool grinding and gave me greater consistency and repeatability of tool bevels. My system is shown in **Figure 4-11**. The basic Wolverine grinding jig comes with two bases. By mounting one under each wheel, grinding operations can be rapidly performed on either side of your grinder without having to re-position bases. The bases are equipped with cam-lock clamping that makes the removal and installation of all attachments easy and quick. The cam forces all attachments rigidly into the base, which eliminates any play.

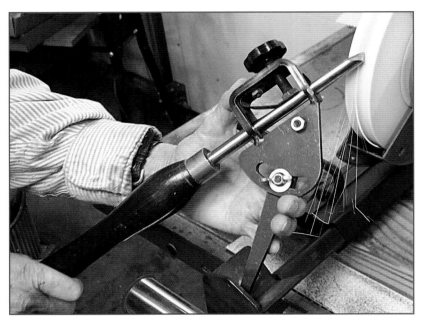

Figure 4-11. This grinder is equipped with the Wolverine grinding jig and Vari-Grind attachment.

This grinding jig also comes equipped with an adjustable platform that has a 3 x 5 inch (75mm x 125mm) working area. This platform can be used on either the left or right sides of the grinder. An adjustable speed handle allows you to make adjustments quickly and ensures that the handle is never in the way. With a grinding jig such as the Wolverine, more consistent grinding will improve your turning because the tools will cut better and will result in fewer digs and produce better results. Gouges are ground in the vee-arm supplied with the Wolverine jig. The vee-arm slides in the base. It is long enough to hold any standard tool. Adjusting the arm is done by unlocking the clamping lever, moving the arm in or out, and re-clamping the lever. Once the proper angle has been established, the tool handle is placed in the vee-pocket and the tool cutting edge is placed directly on the wheel. By simply rolling the tool a perfect bevel is ground. Unfortunately, this produces a square end on your gouges. A popular shape to a bowl

gouge is an "Irish" or "side" grind, **Figure 4-11**. This type of grind is best achieved using their Vari-Grind attachment.

Three gouges that are very popular and useful are the fingernail shape, the traditional bowl gouge, and the side grind configurations. These shapes, however, are difficult to free-hand grind and maintain. The Vari-Grind attachment is designed to properly shape and maintain the edge on standard bowl gouges, the modern side grind (also known as the Ellsworth grind, Liam O'Neil, or Irish grind), and the traditional fingernail shape for spindle work detailing.

To use the Vari-Grind jig, the tool is clamped in the tool holder and the end of the Vari-Grind is placed into the pocket of the vee-arm of the grinding jig. This allows the proper bevel to be set by moving the vee-pocket in or out. This attachment allows complete control of the grind and enables grinds to be easily duplicated.

Q What is the Woodcut Tru-Grind system?

In late 2002, Woodcut 2000 Ltd. of New Zealand brought out their answer to the Oneway Wolverine system. They called it the Tru-Grind tool sharpening system and claimed that it will sharpen all turning tools. The basic system consists of an adjustable base and a tool holder that is similar to the Wolverine Vari-Grind jig. I obtained one of the tools and did a review on it in the December 2002 issue of *More Woodturning*. I found their claim to be true. It is easy to use and it will sharpen all of the woodturning tools, even skew chisels and scrapers. **Figure 4-12** shows the Tru-Grind tool sharpening system in use.

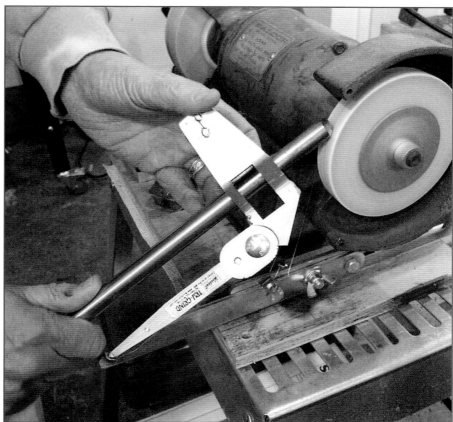

Figure 4-12. The Woodcut Tru-Grind system does a good job of sharpening a gouge.

There are a couple of accessories for the Tru-Grind system that expand its capabilities over any other sharpening system that I've used. One accessory is a scraper tool holder designed to hold the 1/4-inch (6mm) square tool bits used in many of the hollowing systems. Another accessory is the stem sharpener for grinding small, flat cutters typical of those used with many hollowing systems. Both of these accessories are useful when sharpening small cutters that are otherwise difficult to sharpen.

Q What is the Ellsworth grinding jig?

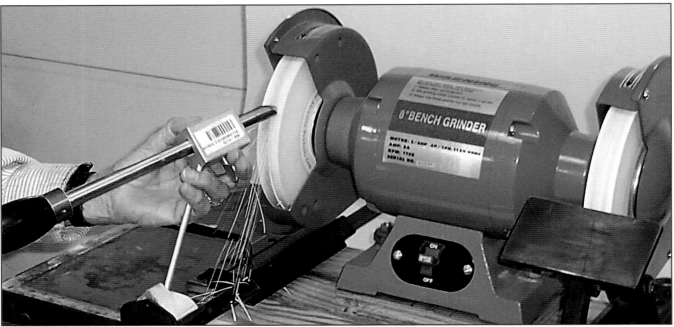

The Ellsworth grinding jig, **Figure 4-13**, is one of the simplest and easiest to use on the market. It consists of a block of aluminum with a square hole through its length and a screw to lock the tool in the jig. A length of steel rod protrudes from the bottom of the block at an angle. This rod fits into a socket in a wooden base that you can make. Since I have the Wolverine system installed on one of my grinders, I simply made a block of wood that would fit into the vee-pocket on my Wolverine that would raise the Ellsworth jig to the proper relationship with the grinding wheel.

Originally, David Ellsworth introduced this jig to his students and guided them in making their own to reproduce his grind. The jig is simplicity itself, but is only designed to grind a 5/8-inch (16mm) gouge and only the swept-back wing style that Ellsworth favors, **Figure 4-14**. Recently, by demand, David had the jig made in aluminum and steel. It is available from several places, including Woodcraft Supply.

I purchased a 1/2-inch (12.5mm) bowl gouge that had the Ellsworth style grind on it. It would

Figure 4-13. The Ellsworth grinding jig can be used with the Wolverine grinding jig to sharpen an Ellsworth style grind on a 5/8-inch (16mm) Ellsworth signature gouge.

not work in the Ellsworth jig directly. I made up a sleeve out of African blackwood that took up the space between the tool and the square hole in the jig. With this adapter, the jig does a perfect grind on my bowl gouge.

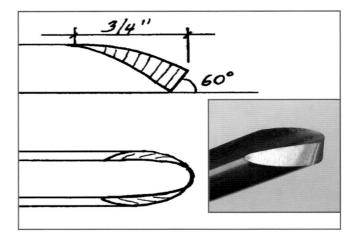

Figure 4-14. The wings of the bowl gouge are swept back in the Ellsworth or Irish grind.

Q What is the Tormek sharpening system?

Geoff Brown of BriMarc Associates, the UK distributor for Tormek tools, gave me a nice two-hour demonstration of the Tormek wet grinder. He was showing me how to grind various tools and I said, "Why not show me on some of my tools?" So he sharpened my Crown 1/2-inch roughing-out gouge and my Crown Pro-PM 3/8-inch bowl gouge, **Figure 4-15**. Neither of these tools had ever been this sharp before.

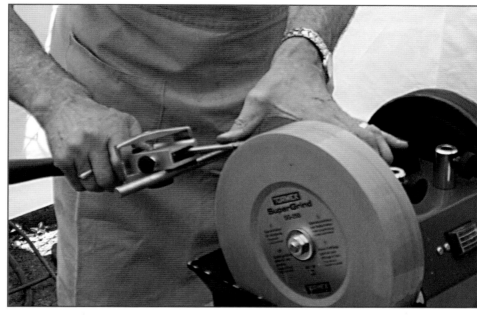

Figure 4-15. The Tormek grinding system uses a wide, soft wheel that turns through a cooling bath of water. The jig mounted on the skew chisel controls the bevel angle.

I told Geoff that I recognized that a tool from the Tormek grinder was going to be sharper than a tool sharpened on my Woodcraft slow speed grinder using the Wolverine system, however, I was not convinced that the sharper edge would give me longer turning time between sharpenings.

Geoff said that one production turner in England, who switched to the Tormek, now sharpens six or seven times a day instead of thirty to forty times a day. It may take longer to sharpen a chisel on the Tormek, but if you can cut the number of sharpenings by that much, the little extra time would make it worth the effort, not only in time saved, but in saved steel.

This grinder works best after you have your tool to shape. When a lot of profiling is required, it's better use a dry grinder with a coarse wheel to do that work, even though you could do it on the Tormek but with a much greater expense of time. Once the profile is set, Tormek recommends that you put a tag on your tool showing what settings are needed, to make the set-up as quick and painless as possible.

I got my Tormek in late October 2000 and used it to sharpen a few of my tools before going to the club exhibition in La Conner, Washington, in early November. Those skews were really sharp. I turned for two days without re-sharpening. I normally have to take my tools home the first night and sharpen them for the next day. I continued to use those tools at home for some time without re-sharpening.

After five years of use, I've still not sharpened all of my tools on the Tormek, but I have sharpened all of those that I use regularly. They do cut much longer than a tool sharpened on a regular dry grinder, though I honestly don't know how much longer. I have found that for those tools for which I've recorded a setting, it takes only a very short time to re-sharpen, probably about the same amount of time as on the dry grinder with a Wolverine jig.

FAQ 5

Wood

Figure 5-1. Bill Tarleton saws a log section into two bowl blanks and removes the pith at the same time.

Q Where do I get wood for turning?

There are three main sources for turning wood: purchased turning blanks, found wood that is dry and cracked, and found wood that is fresh cut, **Figure 5-1**. You may have to purchase wood from any of these sources. The purchased turning blanks require the least effort to get the wood onto the lathe and begin turning. Once your friends and neighbors know that you turn wood, they will often steer you to wood finds or will actually bring wood to you. Such woods generally require the most care and are often badly cracked. They do, however, cost the least of any woods that you may turn. If you obtain fresh cut wood and put it on the shelf to dry, it will take about one year per inch, plus one year, for it to season properly. Rough-turning the item will greatly reduce the amount of time required to dry the wood. I should mention that although you can turn almost any wood, there are a number of woods that are more desirable. A list has been compiled in Appendix C.

Q Can I purchase commercial turning blanks for both bowl and spindle work?

The most common turning blanks available from places serving the woodturning community are a supply of pen blanks, tool handle blanks, regular turning squares for spindle work, and turning squares for bowls (square bowl blanks). When we visited England, we saw many bowl turning blanks that had been sawn round and were ready to mount onto the lathe. An example of this is shown in **Figure 5-2**, which is a photograph of the wood warehouse at Turner's Retreat, a woodturning supply source owned by Robert Sorby in England. Craft Supplies USA in Provo, Utah, carries a good selection of pen blanks, tool handle blanks, baseball bat blanks, and regular turning squares for spindle work and turning squares for bowl work. They also carry some of the specialty woods such as colorwood, color ply blocks and bowl blanks. For people wishing to do segmented work, some sources sell segmented vessel kits with the wood cut and ready to be glued up and turned. This is one form of turning in which flat boards, which are generally available at many lumber yards, can be used. Also, if one has one of the ring-cutting tools, flat boards can be made into very nice bowl blanks. The advantage of purchasing prepared turning blanks is that you require

Figure 5-2. These commercial turning blanks sit on the shelf at a supplier.

less auxiliary equipment to be able to start turning. The disadvantage is the cost of the wood. Working with found wood requires one to own a chainsaw and a band saw to process the wood; however, these tools will be paid for rather quickly from the savings resulting from using free found wood.

Q   Where do I get dry and cracked wood?

The best place to get dry cracked wood is out of someone's firewood pile. In many cases very good turning wood is simply split and used for fuel in a wood stove or fireplace. This wood is not generally sealed on the end grain to reduce or prevent splitting and will therefore have many checks and cracks in it. The wood stacked outside of our regular storage shed is from two trees that had to be removed as a result of progress. These two 40 year-old trees, an elm and a butternut, had to be cut in our neighbor's yard because of a change in the road in front of their home. We obtained the wood in exchange for a nice bowl and a few hours of woodturning training. We selected the choice pieces for our turning wood storage and then split the rest for firewood. This is a very common practice and a good source for turning wood. If you don't have a firewood pile, ask your neighbors to let you look through theirs. I once obtained some very fine hard maple and madrone from a relative's firewood pile. The wood had lots of cracks, but was very dry and ready to turn. They were happy to get a turned bowl in return for the wood and I had many hours of enjoyment turning that wood into all sorts of items.

Q   Where do I get fresh-cut wood?

Fresh-cut wood is available everywhere: along the road where road crews have taken out trees, after storms when trees have been blown down or severely damaged, construction sites where trees are being removed to make room for new homes, and tree removal services. This is where you need your own chain saw. These trees have to be cut up into suitable lengths for woodturning. That work is best done with a chainsaw, **Figure 5-1** on page 50.

Q   How do I cut the wood for turning?

It is a good practice to cut the wood for turning into turning blanks that are slightly oversize to allow for the inevitable end-grain checking that often occurs even when it has been sealed with a green-wood sealer. Depending upon the size of the tree and how much of it you have permission to use, it may be desirable to have some of the tree trunk sawn into lumber of different thicknesses. This is especially true if you also make furniture and other items besides bowls and hollow forms. This is best done by a band saw mills or a sawyer if you can find one who will handle single tree lots.

The trunk sections should be cut into lengths that are about 2 inches longer than they are in diameter. These pieces should then be cut to remove the pith. The pith or center of the trunk is where most cracking originates. With this removed, the likelihood of cracks is diminished. If the tree is small (under 12 inches (300mm) in diameter), generally you can use a chainsaw to cut down through the pith. This will remove the pith and leave you two halves that can be used for bowls. The normal orientation of these half-log chunks is to put the top of the bowl at the flat sawn area where you cut out the pith. This provides a nice, smooth-top bowl for salads and other utility uses. Making the top of the bowl to be the bark side of the blank will give you a natural edge bowl, which falls into the decorative category not generally used for food.

Figure 5-1 on page 50 shows Bill Tarleton sawing a tree section into two bowl blanks and removing the pith at the same time. When the tree is large, over 14 inches (350mm) in diameter, it is a good idea to remove the pith as a slice of wood that may be used for some other purpose. The log section may then be cut into several bowl blanks of various thicknesses and diameters. When cutting up large tree sections such as this, it helps to have a chain saw with a bar that is longer than the piece of wood. It is then possible to make several cuts part way through while the log section is mounted on a secure foundation. As soon as possible after cutting this wood, within minutes if possible, you must seal the end grain of the blanks and get them out of the sun. For more information on cutting timber, see *Harvesting Urban Timber* by Sam Sherrill (Linden Publishing).

Q How do I seal the end grain to prevent cracking?

Anchor Seal is one of the best wood sealers that I've found. It is a water/wax emulsion that you can paint onto the end grain of the wood. When the water evaporates, it leaves a wax coating that seals the end grain and slows the drying .

You can also melt a large amount of sealing wax and dip the end grain into the hot wax. This method works well on small sections of wood but not so well on bowl blanks because the amount of wax required would be dangerously large. Many people claim that old latex paint works very well as an end grain sealer; I've never tried it. One turner that I know uses Liquid Nails for wet wood. He says it is the best sealer he has ever used. He turns large bowls (2 feet (600mm) to 4 feet (1200mm) diameters) and has been turning for about 40 years. Whenever it is possible, it is a good idea to rough-turn the item, then seal the end grain. A rough-turned bowl may be dry in three months to one year instead of four or five years.

Q What do you mean by rough-turning and what can I rough-turn?

Bowls, little boxes, and hollow forms are the most common items that are rough-turned from fresh-cut wood to help speed the drying process and help reduce the amount of cracking. As shown in **Figure 5-3**, rough-turned bowls are generally turned to a wall thickness of about 10 percent of the diameter, that is, a 10-inch (250mm) bowl will be roughed to a 1-inch (25mm) wall thickness. Such a bowl will normally dry within three months depending upon how you store it. Little boxes can be rough turned and then taped together with the hollowed portions open to the air. This is good even if your wood is supposedly dry. Rough-turn it a few days before final turning. This allows the wood to express itself before you final-turn and fit the lid.

Hollow forms and little boxes are normally turned in spindle mode with the grain running parallel to the axis of rotation. As a result they do not warp out of round as much as a bowl will because the bowl has both side grain and end grain in its diameter. A 10 percent wall thickness would still be safe.

Figure 5-3. This bowl has been rough-turned. The Woodcut bowl saver has been used to cut the center from the bowl, thus reducing the amount of shavings needing to be removed from the shop.

Q How do I dry my wood?

Drying is the part of collecting wood for turning that can be most destructive to the turning blanks and disappointing to the collector. There are two options for the turner. You can seal the wood and store it on a shelf out of the weather and sun and allow it to dry slowly, or you can rough-turn the wood to a 10 percent wall thickness and place it on the shelf to dry using one of several methods available.

Q How do I store my wood as solid turning blanks?

Assuming that you have cut the wood into turning blanks as previously described, the wood should have its end grain sealed and should then be stored on a shelf with wooden stickers. The stickers are strips of wood about 1/4 inch (6mm) thick and up to 1-1/2 (40mm) inches wide. I've found that old lath can be used as stickers. The stickers separate the blanks so that air can flow all around the wood, as shown in **Figure 5-4**. Drying occurs best when the wood is stored out of the weather and sunshine, but where it can get sufficient airflow to carry away the moisture. Every species of wood behaves differently when seasoning. Some of the most difficult to season properly are the fruit woods. Madrone is also very difficult to season.

Figure 5-4. These bowl blanks have their ends sealed to retard checking and cracking.

Q How do I dry rough-turned projects?

Figure 5-5. After drying, this rough-turned bowl is ready to final turn.

Richard Raffan says that he tosses his newly turned wet wood bowls into a pile and allows them to air dry for a day or two. He then puts them into cardboard boxes and puts them on the shelf to finish drying. He writes the date on the box and waits up to a year before he final-turns the bowls in the box. During the drying process, the bowl will warp and sometimes crack. **Figure 5-5** shows a rough turned and warped bowl. I assume that the box keeps air from drying the bowls too quickly and the cardboard may absorb some of the moisture. I've had very good luck putting rough turned bowls into old paper grocery sacks and placing them on the shelf. There are several other methods that people are using to dry bowls and keep them from cracking, namely, microwave drying, boiling, soaking in dish detergent mixture, and soaking in alcohol. I've tried all of these with fair results. I recently heard another theory on drying that violates all of the rules.

This fellow says that an old logger friend told him about this method. Dry the wood while it stands vertically as the tree grew. He says that there is minimal checking, and warping is kept to a minimum. I think he was drying boards, rather than bowl blanks, but it is worth trying.

Q   What is this paper bag method?

In the paper bag method, you simply finish turning the piece and place it into a brown grocery bag, seal the opening, and place on a shelf to dry. It will generally take from three to six months depending upon the type of wood. I've used a slight variation of this in which I placed some of the shavings from the bowl into the bag, filled the interior of the bowl with

shavings and placed it into the bag, and added a few more shavings. The bag was then sealed and left on the shelf for a couple of weeks. I then removed the bowl from the bag and placed it on the shelf to air dry without any other protection. Either method seems to work well on most woods. Write the date that the bowl was turned and the type of wood for future reference.

Q   What is the boiling method?

I can't tell you what boiling does to the wood, but it makes it dry more quickly and it turns better after boiling. For woods like madrone and many of the fruit woods, boiling is nearly the only way to dry them without massive cracking. Most woods can be boiled for one to two hours with good results. Madrone may take eight hours of boiling to make it safe for drying.

To boil a rough-turned bowl, you need a kettle that the bowl will fit into. Cover it with water but allowed to float with the hollowed side up and full of water. Bring the water to a boil and then let it cook for two hours. Then submerge

the bowl in a cool water bath for a few minutes.

In many cases, I've been able to final-turn a bowl blank within a month after it was boiled. They often do not warp very much. I had a 10 inch (250mm) apple wood bowl that only warped about 1/16 inch (2mm) after boiling and the wood turned with very fine long shavings. It was impressive. We have not had such good luck with all boiled bowls, however. Some have warped and cracked as they dried. Apparently, we had not relieved all stresses in the wood during boiling. However, we've had mold on virtually all bowls that we've boiled.

Q   What is freezing?

Another method that my wife and I have often used is freezing. You place the rough-turned bowl into the freezer for a couple of days. You then place the frozen bowl into the refrigerator for a few weeks. The freezing apparently damages the cells of the wood and the defrost

cycle of the refrigerator sucks out the moisture. We heard about this method from Australian turners and have had fair success with it. Unfortunately, our freezer is too full of food to do this much. It seems to work, but I've not found anyone who could explain why.

Q What is microwave drying?

When time is short and you just have to finish your bowl, the microwave becomes a viable method. The normally accepted practice is to put the bowl in a brown paper bag and place it in the microwave. Using the defrost setting, give the bowl one to three minutes. Remove the bowl from the microwave and from the brown paper bag. Allow it to completely cool. Then repeat this process until the bowl is dry.

If you have a moisture meter, you can check for dryness. The less expensive method is to weigh the bowl before the first heat and then weigh it again after each heat. When the weight doesn't change from the previous heating, the bowl is dry. This may take several trips to the microwave, but make sure that the wood doesn't become too dry and cause a fire. Smoke in the kitchen doesn't endear one to the cook.

Q What is the soaking in dish detergent thing?

I've not had much luck with soaking rough-turned bowls in a solution of dish detergent and water. Supposedly, it does work and many people use the process and claim fantastic success. I think they use a mixture of about 1:6 detergent and water. The bowl is submerged for a one to three days and then removed and allowed to dry until it is ready for final turning. Some people report little warping and no cracking. They also say that the wood turns significantly better after being soaked in the detergent solution. We tried this on a few different types of wood: plum (with massive warping and cracking), and aspen and willow with great results (little warping, no cracking, and turning was greatly improved).

Q What about using alcohol to dry wood?

At the time of this writing, I have had limited experience with the alcohol method of drying wood. However, Dave Smith did an article for the November 2004 issue of *More Woodturning* that described his success with soaking rough-turned bowls in alcohol for one to two hours or even overnight. He had several others try his method with good results before announcing it to the public. Dave said that he had soaked a bowl in alcohol for two hours, wrapped it in brown grocery bag paper, taping it at the rim, and leaving the inside or hollow open to the air. In seven days, he said it was ready to final turn. However, he was turning small bowls that had wall thicknesses of 1/4 inch (6mm) to 3/8 inch (10mm). Seven days might be a bit short for a salad bowl having a 1-1/2 inch (40mm) thick wall. We tried this successfully on several maple bowls and one madrone bowl. They were dry and ready to final turn in about seven days. All warped, but did not crack.

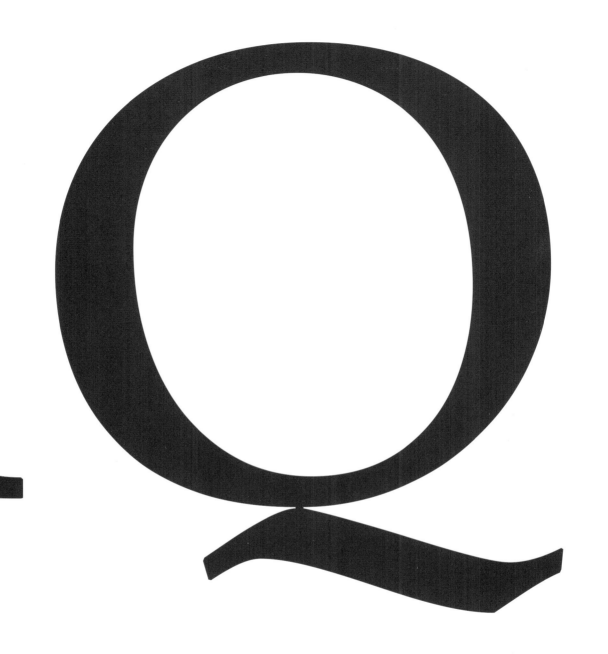

Part II—What Do I turn?

FAQ 6
Spindle Turning

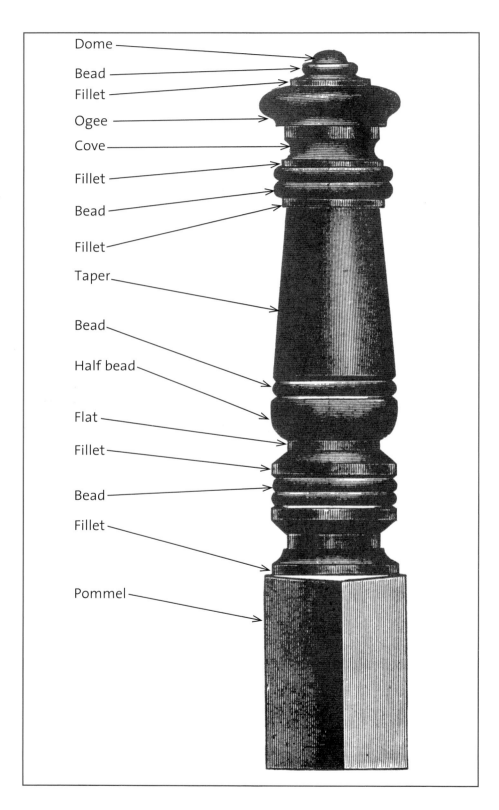

Dome
Bead
Fillet
Ogee
Cove
Fillet
Bead
Fillet
Taper
Bead
Half bead
Flat
Fillet
Bead
Fillet
Pommel

Figure 6-1. The parts of a spindle. This spindle was available in the 1893 Blumer and Kuhn Catalog of Premium Mill Work as newel post number 1328.

Q What is a spindle?

A spindle is a piece of wood that has been turned round with the grain running parallel to the axis of rotation of the lathe. This piece of wood may be simple in form like the common dowel that we can buy in the hardware store or it may have some specific shape such as a baseball bat. Normally, spindles will have some function such as a chair leg, table leg, stairway spindle, or newel post. Each spindle, no matter how ornate, will generally have up to three different shapes included in its turning, namely, the bead, the cove, and the flat area or fillet. Other shapes are generally a combination of these three. For example, the ogee is a combination of half a bead and half a cove joined by a small fillet. **Figure 6-1** shows a spindle with several shapes and identifies each of the shapes. In the following pages we will discuss how each of these shapes are formed.

Q How do I turn a bead?

The bead can be made by a variety of turning tools. It is essentially one-half of a sphere in cross section. One of the most common tools used by experienced turners is the skew chisel. However, many choose the beading and parting tool, which is sharpened much like the skew chisel except its cutting edge is not skewed. The beading and parting tool is made from square cross-section steel, but has a bevel cut on two sides so that the cutting edge is located at the center of the stock. If your bead must be a specific size, there are beading tools on the market for different widths of beads. The spindle detail gouge can make a decent bead and the Bill Jones point tool can also make fine beads in harder woods. **Figure 6-2** shows a number of beads on a spindle. Each bead was turned with a different tool.

For this discussion, we will use the skew chisel. Begin by laying out the width of the bead by cutting V grooves on each side of the bead. To do this, push the long point of the skew chisel into the wood with the long point down and the short point directly above it. Hold the tool shaft as near 90 degrees to the rotating wood as possible. Bring the tool back and tilt it a few degrees to either the left or right then make a slicing cut down into the original cut. Tilt the tool to the other side a few degrees and repeat this cut. You should

Figure 6-2. These three beads were cut with a skew.

now have a good sharp V cut. Repeat on the other side of the bead location.

With a pencil, mark the center line of the bead to be turned. Now, with the skew rotated on its side, the short point facing the direction of cut, and the tool shank as near 90 degrees to the rotating wood, the short point should be just to the left of the center line. Lift the handle slightly so that the short point will cut and rotate the tool handle to the left or counter-clockwise. The cut should proceed in an arc so that when the tool has been rotated 90 degrees, the short point of the skew hits the bottom of the V cut. Repeat for the other side and you will have a finished bead. When done, the pencil center line should still be on the top of the bead.

Q How do I make a cove?

The detail spindle gouge is the tool of choice to make a cove, which is sort of a mirror image of a bead in cross section. It is a depression cut into the wood, often quite U shaped in cross section. In very hard woods, a small round-nose scraper can do a very nice job of making coves. I should mention two other tools that will also do a fine job of making coves: the Skewchigouge made by Crown Tools, and the Spindle Master made by Robert Sorby. **Figure 6-3** shows a series of coves of different widths.

Begin to make your cove by laying out its location and width on a spindle that has already been turned round, **Figure 6-4**. Then, with the spindle gouge, cut down into the area of the cove, but only cut halfway, **Figure 6-5**. Reverse your cut to come from the other side and meet your previous cut at the middle of the cove, **Figure 6-6**. Never try to cut uphill from the bottom of the cove. The grain wants to be cut downhill so that the fibers that you are cutting are supported by fibers below. If you try to cut uphill, your tool will tear out fibers that were unsupported and leave a rough surface. It takes practice to make the right and left cuts so that they cut cleanly to the bottom of the cove, but it can be done.

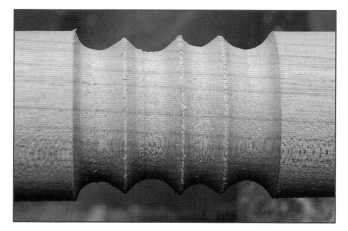

Figure 6-3. Here are various coves of different widths.

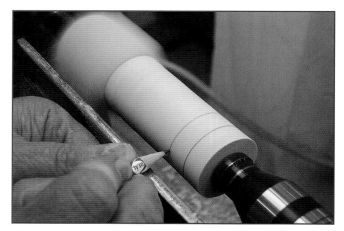

Figure 6-4. Lay out the cove on a spindle by marking where it begins and ends.

Figure 6-5. Make the first cut on the cove from the right side.

Figure 6-6. Make the finishing cut from the left side of the cove.

Q Why a flat area on a spindle?

Flat areas on spindles generally are transitions between other shapes. A short flat area separating two different shapes is called a fillet. It is generally a very narrow flat area and it is generally parallel to the axis of rotation. On chair spindles there may be a long flat area that separates some decoration on each end of the spindle, such as a bead just before the joining tenon, which is another flat area. **Figure 6-7** shows how the flat areas on a spindle are used to separate the different decorations.

The flat areas on a spindle are generally made with a skew chisel; however, short flat areas or fillets are often turned with a good sharp parting tool having about the same width as the fillet. The skew chisel is normally used like a plane to smooth the flat surface, **Figure 6-8**. The skew is used with the short point leading and all cutting being done with the lower part of the cutting edge. If you allow the cut to move above center of the cutting edge, there will be a catch that will cut decorative spirals that you don't want along your nice flat area.

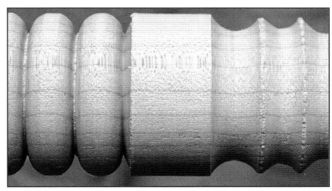

Figure 6-7. Flat areas or fillets on a spindle are used to separate the different decorations.

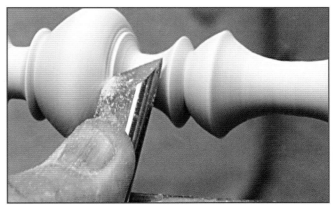

Figure 6-8. Use the corner of the skew to plane a fillet smooth.

Q What is an ogee and how is it made?

The ogee is the combination of two different shapes: one-half of a bead and one-half of a cove. Two tools are normally used to make ogees: the skew chisel to make the one-half of a bead, and the detail spindle gouge completes the task by making the one-half of a cove. The spindle gouge can be used to make the complete shape. The Skewchigouge, made by Crown Tools, and the Spindle Master, made by Robert Sorby, can also be used to make the complete ogee. An ogee is shown in **Figure 6-9**.

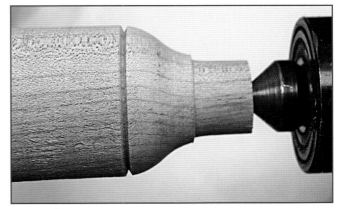

Figure 6-9. The ogee combines half a bead and half a cove.

Q I want to turn a table leg, how do I proceed?

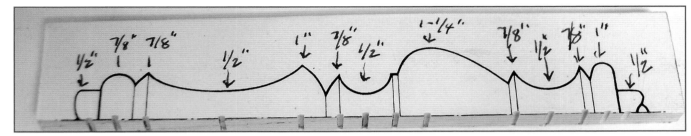

Figure 6-10. A notched story-stick helps mark spindles for turning.

A table leg usually has a top part that is square. If it is a long, thin table leg you will need at least one center steady to reduce the whip and spiraling chatter as you move away from the headstock or tailstock. You have four problems if you are making, four legs that you wish to be the same. If you are only making a single replacement piece the problem is a bit simpler.

Make a story stick, that is, a straight stick with the high and low points marked on it with reference from one end of the leg, **Figure 6-10**. Cut little notches in the stick at the pencil marks so that you can lay the stick alongside the blank and transfer these points. At each mark on the stick, write the diameter so you can set a spring caliper to the dimension, **Figure 6-11**. Then use a parting tool and the spring caliper to cut the spindle down to that diameter. Once all the points have been marked and turned down, you are ready to shape the leg.

If you are making a new table leg, make a drawing of the shape of the table leg and transfer it to a piece of stiff cardboard or 1/4-inch (6mm) plywood. This template can then be used to check the shape as you turn.

The one difference between a table leg and other turned spindles is the square section at the top of the leg, called a pommel, and the transition from square to round. Turn all of the round part until it is clean and round. Then with the spindle running at a reasonably high speed, use the long point of the skew chisel to turn half a bead that starts on the square part and ends at the rounded part, see **Figure 6-12**

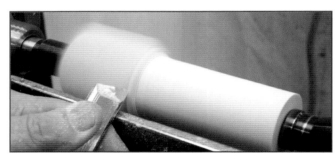

Figure 6-11. Use calipers and a parting tool to mark the high and low points on the spindle.

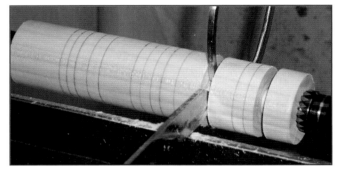

Figure 6-12. Use the long point of the skew to turn the transition from square to round on a table leg.

Figure 6-13. The transition from square to round should be clean and sharp.

and **Figure 6-13**. If you are reproducing a table leg, you will have to make this transition match the other table legs.

Q How do I turn a lamp?

Most turned lamps consist of at least two parts. The upright is generally spindle-turned to some pleasing shape. The base is normally faceplate turned, that is, the grain runs perpendicular to the axis of rotation. **Figure 6-14** shows the components of a lamp.

There is one difference between a lamp and other spindles. That difference is the hole needed for the electrical cord. There are a number of ways to get this hole through the upright part. One way is to make that part from a glue-up in which you have left a hole through the center. You then mount the spindle with those holes being the center on each end. Another way is to use a lamp auger, see **Figure 6-15**, to drill the hole while the wood is mounted on the lathe. To do this, your lathe must have a bored-through tailstock and a bored-through headstock. This way you can bore half way from either end, hoping that the holes will meet in the center. You can drill the hole before you turn the spindle. If you do so, you will need to plug the holes so that your lathe centers can be centered on the holes.

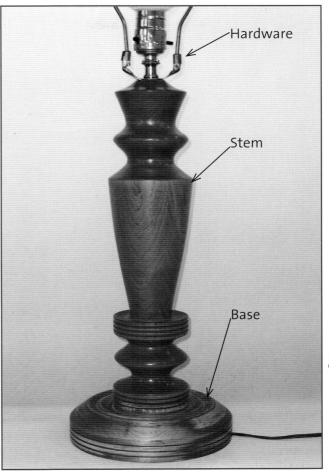

Figure 6-14. A turned lamp has these parts.

Figure 6-15. A lamp auger has a special end on it, which enables it to drill the hole without wandering off center.

Q I am considering doing architectural turning, what is involved?

Architectural turning is one area of turning in which a person may be able to make a good living. It does, however, require a heavy duty lathe with a lot of distance between centers. You may well need one or more center steadies on very long pieces. Two items that come to mind are newel posts for stairways, especially where the architect has specified that the newel posts be different from any commercially available, and pillars or columns where the turning stock must be fabricated to reduce the weight of the finished turning.

Q How do I turn a newel post?

Figure 6-16. This newel post was turned during a demonstration at the Utah Woodturning Symposium.

One set of newel posts that I turned a few years ago were for a specially designed stairway which required that every newel post have a light on top. In addition, the ground-level newel post was in the shape of a lighthouse. I had 48 inches (1200mm) between centers on my lathe. I discovered that was not enough to handle any of these posts. I found it was necessary to turn the regular newel posts in two pieces, I joined them at a bead so that the joint was hidden. The lighthouse newel post had to be turned in four pieces because a wood carver was going to hollow out the light area. These were made from recycled old-growth fir. The stock measured 5 inches (125mm) square and was a real load for my lathe. The customer furnished the wood. Most newel posts will not be this difficult and 48 inches (1200mm) between centers might handle them. A newel post being turned is shown in Figure 6-16.

Q What about the composition of the stock for large turnings?

Figure 6-17. This 18-inch (450mm) by 9-foot 6-inch (2900mm) column has been made up by stave construction and is ready to turn in Art Ransom's shop.

Most very large turnings are made from fabricated stock. The process is known as stave construction. The number of sides required depends upon the thickness of the wood being used for the fabrication and the diameter of the finished spindle. **Figure 6-17** shows the method of joining the woods together for stave construction. One must make a scale drawing of a cross-section of the pillar. If the pillar is tapered, then a scale drawing must be made of each end of the tapered area. The boards in that case must be cut not only at an angle for joining but also tapered to cover the transition from the large diameter to the smaller diameter.

Once the piece has been glued up for turning, it is necessary to make end pieces for the centers of the lathe to fit into. These can be as simple as a wooden disk sawn from a heavy piece of wood and attached to the end of the turning blank with screws. The center of this must be marked very precisely. Since the inside is hollow, you do not want to turn off center and make a hole in the side of the pillar. On the drive end of this pillar, I recommend that you drill a hole the diameter of the drive center that is about 1/2 inch (12mm) deep, to keep the center from slipping to the side and off of the end. It would be a good idea to do this on the tail center end as well for the same reason.

FAQ 7

Bowl Turning

Figure 7-1. A bowl blank is mounted on the lathe between centers, ready to turn the outside and the foot of the bowl.

Q How do I turn a bowl?

There are almost as many ways to turn a bowl as there are bowl turners. Perhaps the method used by many beginners, who have only a faceplate on which to mount their wood, could be considered the simplest. For this method, the bowl is mounted to the faceplate on the foot side of the bowl blank and the entire bowl is turned inside and out to completion. It is then removed from the faceplate, the base is sanded, and the holes are plugged by some means. If you do not have a chuck, this may be your method for mounting your wood to turn a bowl. I have found, however, that it is better to mount the wood three different times when turning a bowl: once to turn the outside and the foot of the bowl, once to turn the inside of the bowl, and a final mounting to finish the foot of the bowl. This is the method I will describe in the following paragraphs.

Mount the bowl blank with the top facing the headstock. You can mount this on a screw chuck, on a faceplate, or between centers as shown in **Figure 7-1**. For many years, I used a screw chuck on the top side of the bowl to turn the outside and foot of the bowl, but have found that a bowl blank mounted between centers gives me more flexibility in mounting to take advantage of the grain of the wood. Actually, I now mount the blank between the open jaws of the four-jaw chuck and a live cup tail center, instead of between centers.

For utilitarian type bowls, the foot should be about 1/3 to 1/2 of the diameter of the finished bowl. Use a bowl gouge work the wood into the desired bowl shape, cutting from the foot toward the top of the bowl. This method allows the fibers of wood to be supported best for cutting. Shape the foot to prepare it for mounting when the bowl is reversed to hollow the inside. Sand and finish the outside of the bowl before reversing to hollow the inside.

If you do not have a chuck to grip the foot

Figure 7-2. The bowl has been reversed and held in a chuck to hollow its inside.

while turning the inside, you will need to mount a waste block onto your faceplate and turn a recess in the waste block to fit the foot of the bowl. You can make this a snug enough fit to serve as a jam-fit chuck and then simply turn the inside of the bowl on this mounting. You could also glue the foot into the recess in the waste block to give you a more secure mounting. I prefer to use a chuck, **Figure 7-2**.

With the bowl mounted on its foot, true up the top surface of the bowl with scraping cuts taken from the center of the bowl to the outside rim. It is important to smooth the face of the bowl to prevent grabs of your tool as you start to enter the wood. The proper way to cut the inside of the bowl is from the outside edge towards the center. I generally start near the center of the bowl blank and cut in with a scooping cut to start hollowing. You may also drill a hole to approximately the same depth that you plan to hollow the bowl. You then cut into the drilled hole and work back toward the outside as the recess deepens. If the bowl is to have a very thin wall, it is best to finish-turn the wall as the hollowing deepens, to avoid the flexing that will occur on thin-walled bowls as the recess becomes deeper.

The wall will generally cut nicely down the side, but will begin to give you trouble as you near the bottom. The bevel of the tool will no longer rub the wood as you reach that transition point. You then need a second gouge with a steeper bevel, say 60 to 80 degrees, to cut across the bottom of the bowl. Alternatively, you can cut back from the center of the bowl to meet the transition point and then finally finish with very light cuts using a heavy duty round-nose scraper. Finally, sand through the grits to finish the inside of the bowl. You may at this point apply your finish to the inside. It is now ready to reverse again to turn the foot.

There are many ways to hold the bowl while the foot is finished. The simplest method is to mount a disk of wood on a faceplate and cut a recess in the disk to fit the top of your bowl. You may then hold the bowl in place while turning the foot with the tail center. This will leave you a small piece that must be carved away and then sanded smooth.

Other methods of holding a bowl while turning the foot, include a set of large jaws for your

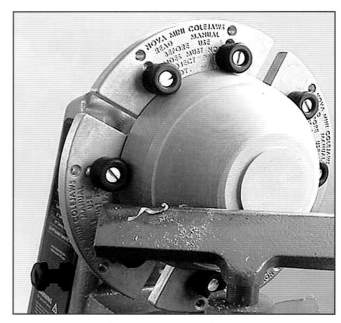

Figure 7-3. The bowl has again been reversed to finish the foot. It is being held in large jaws known as Cole jaws.

chuck (**Figure 7-3**), a Longworth chuck, a domed piece of wood on a faceplate with a cushioning material between the dome and the inside of the bowl, and finally the newest and best method, the vacuum chuck.

The foregoing is applicable to almost any plain bowl that has a smooth top rim. A natural edge bowl requires some differences in handling.

Q What is a natural-edge bowl?

On a natural-edge bowl, the top of the bowl is the outside of the tree, as shown in **Figure 7-4**. The top rim of the bowl will be determined by the shape of the outside of the tree and will normally have the bark remaining on the wood. Thus the top edge of the bowl may vary considerably depending upon the outside of the tree from which it was taken.

The actual turning of a natural-edge bowl does not differ greatly from the turning of a bowl with a normal rim. The primary difference is in starting out to ensure that the two low edges are at about the same height and the two high

Figure 7-4. This is how the natural-edge bowl comes from the log.

edges are near the same height. This is done while the bowl blank is mounted between centers. You turn the outside round and then check the height of the high and low points by drawing pencil lines around the bowl as you turn it by hand. The headstock drive and the tailstock center are then shifted as necessary to obtain the best balance, before you final-turn the outside. This sometimes takes several attempts to make it work best for a particular piece of wood. Now, final-turn the outside, taking care as you approach the bark edge. It is sometimes best to cut the bark edge from the top to meet the cut from the bottom. If you cut from the foot toward the rim all the way, you may knock off the bark or tear out the top edge.

When hollowing the bowl, you have a more difficult job because the tool is cutting air much of the time. Some people use a sharp parting tool to cut through the high points and get close to the side of the bowl. This gives a point for the gouge to start cutting without knocking off the bark. The natural-edge bowl is fun to turn and eye-catching when finished, **Figure 7-5** and **Figure 7-6**.

Figure 7-5. The rim of the natural-edge bowl is the bark side of the tree.

Figure 7-6. The interplay of bark, sapwood, and heartwood is fascinating in natural edge bowls.

Figure 7-7. The center of the tree is the opening of this plain-edge bowl.

Q What is a plain bowl and how does it come out of the log?

As shown in **Figure 7-7** and **Figure 7-8**, the top of the plain bowl is at the center of the log. The outside shape of the bowl will be somewhat defined by the outside of the log from which it is taken. If the log is very large, the shape of the bowl is simply determined by the woodturner. However, on smaller logs an uneven surface or depressions can greatly affect the final shape of a bowl.

The rim of a plain bowl can take on several different shapes. My preferred shape for large bowls is a rounded over rim, as shown in **Figure 7-9**. There are some other shapes such as coming to a point, a bevel from the top toward the outside, a flat and wide rim on which decoration may be placed, or a rolled-in top edge.

Figure 7-8. This is how a normal, plain-edge bowl comes from the log.

Figure 7-9. Richard Miller turned a rolled, or undercut, edge on this large bowl..

Q   What is a rolled-edge bowl and how is it different?

A rolled-edge bowl is almost like a shallow hollow form, **Figure 7.9**. The rolled-in edge and the undercut rim give the bowl a very different appearance and is preferred by some woodturners. The outside part is not too difficult to handle. The undercutting is more difficult, because most normal turning tools do not enable you to undercut the rolled-in rim. This is best done with some of the hollowing tools for vases, which allow undercutting because of their shape. Crown Tools also has a tool specifically designed to do this job and it does it very well, see **Figure 7-10**.

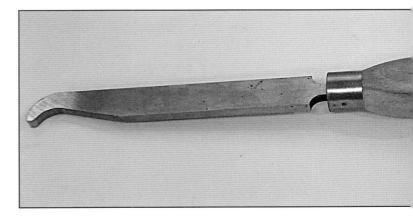

Figure 7-10. The Crown tool is for cutting under the rim on a rolled-edge bowl.

Q I read somewhere about bowls being made from stacked rings, how is this done?

The process of making a bowl from laminated or stacked rings is interesting. The process does limit the shape of the bowl somewhat because the rings are normally cut from a single board with the cuts made at an angle so that the pieces may be stacked in reverse order and glued together to form a bowl shape. If you use several boards and vary the widths of the rings, you can make bowls of different shapes.

The normal process is to use a single piece of wood and cut the rings as shown in **Figure 7-11**. This cutting is done with a thin parting tool held at a specific angle so that the rings will stack properly. Some people cut the board in half and then cut the half-rings with a band saw and glue them together after sawing. Tools to help in this process include the Ring Master, made in the United States, and a Marrison System ring-cutting jig sold by Craft Supplies Ltd. in England. These systems are designed to cut the rings from a solid board. I recently saw a demonstration in which the rings were cut with a thin parting tool. The demonstrator made the cuts at a 45 degree angle and used a backing board to prevent tear-out as the tool cut through. He spaced the cuts apart by the thickness of the board.

This system allows one to make bowls from a single flat board. The bowls in **Figure 7-12** and **Figure 13** are just such bowls. One can enhance the bowl by making the board from segmented pieces and then cutting rings from the segmented board.

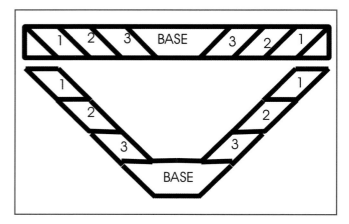

Figure 7-11. Here's how to cut rings from a flat board and glue them into a bowl blank.

Figure 7-12. The rings are glued up and ready to final-turn into a bowl.

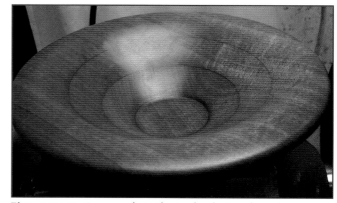

Figure 7-13. A completed stacked-ring bowl.

Q I saw a stack of nested bowls, How is that done?

Nested bowls, **Figure 7-14**, are made from a single turning blank using one of the coring tools: the McNaughton Centre Saver, the Woodcut Bowl Saver, or the Oneway Coring System. Mike Mahoney used the McNaughton Centre Saver, see **Figure 7-15**. This system was originally designed as a center saver so that several bowls could be turned from a single piece of wood. However, it is also useful for mirror or picture frames and rings for inlays and nests of bowls from a single blank. The system's curved radius blades also can produce multi-walled or captive vessels.

The system is quick and easy to assemble; the blades last a long time; it can save centers up to 18 inches (450mm) in diameter; work can be secured with the tailstock; the system can be used for regular parting, and it allows maximum yield from exotic or unusual woods.

Figure 7-16 shows the tool in operation removing the first of several marked cores for a set of nesting bowls.

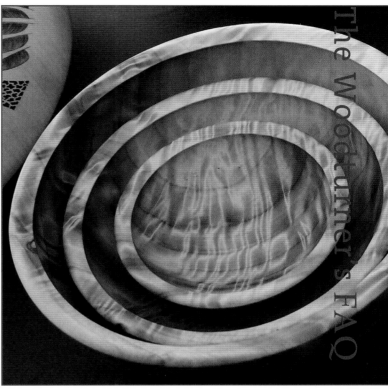
Figure 7-14. Nested bowls by Mike Mahoney.

Figure 7-15. The McNaughton system includes several sizes of cutting tools, plus a handle and a special tool rest.

Figure 7-16. Cutting the first core from a green-wood bowl blank.

Q What is segmented turning and how are segmented bowls made?

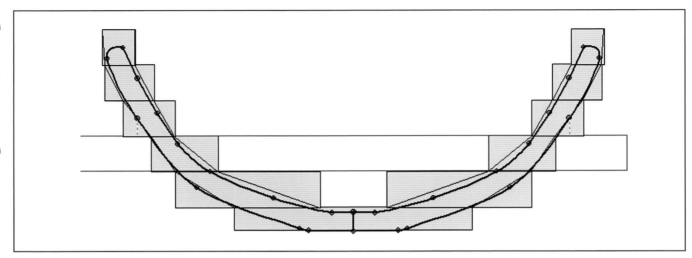

Figure 7-17. This drawing shows how the segmented rings are stacked to make up a bowl blank.

Segmented turning is a way to make a bowl or hollow form out of a number of narrow boards. When I first started turning, I did not have any pieces of wood large enough to make bowls. I did have on hand several feet of 1 inch by 2 inch (25mm x 50mm) pine boards. They became the material for my early bowls. I used segmented turning for most of my early bowls.

Segmented turning is the process by which a number of wedge-shaped pieces are fitted together to form a ring, as shown in **Figure 7-17**. The number of segments in a ring determines the angle of the cut for the wedge-shaped pieces. The formula for determining the angle of cut on these segments is 360 degrees divided by the number of segments divided by two. For example, a ring with eight segments would have 360 degrees divided by eight equals 45

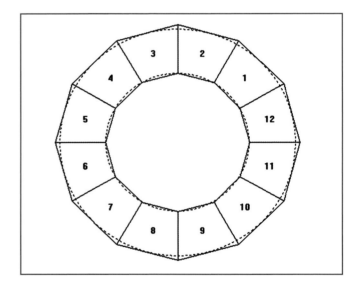

Figure 7-18. Segmented bowls are made up of rings of wood that consist of numerous wedge-shaped pieces.

Figure 7-19. This segmented piece was created by Fred Allen and exhibited at the Utah Woodturning Symposium.

Figure 7-20. This segmented piece was created by Nelson Cassinger and exhibited at the Utah Woodturning Symposium.

degrees included angle for the segment. Divide this by two to obtain a cut angle of 22-1/2 degrees. A sled is generally used on table saws to cut the segments, but chop saws also can be used, as can the band saw.

The number of rings required to make an individual bowl or hollow form and the overall size of the rings is determined by making a drawing of the planned project, including wall thickness. The drawing helps you decide what thickness of boards will be used to make the rings. Parallel lines, starting with the base, are made that thickness apart across the drawing. One can now measure the width of the outside and inside of the vessel wall at each ring. A drawing is then made of two concentric circles to show the finished wall thickness for that ring. Enough width must now be included to make sure there is enough material when

turned to accommodate the wall thickness.

The pieces are fitted together and glued. Titebond II is my choice of glue for the task. A hose clamp of the proper size is generally used to clamp the segments during gluing. A number of rings of different sizes are made up. Each of the rings is then trued on both surfaces. The rings are then stacked and glued together, as shown in **Figure 7-17,** to form the general shape of a bowl or vessel.

Many variations can be used to make some very beautiful bowls and hollow forms by combining different colored woods, as shown in **Figure 7-19** and **Figure 7-20**. There are several good books on the market and several computer programs to aid in the design and construction of segmented bowls and vessels. They are listed in Appendix A.

Q What's involved in reverse turning to finish the foot of a bowl?

I touched on this briefly earlier in the chapter when talking about the basic method in which bowls are turned. I stated that each bowl I turn is mounted three different ways: once to turn the outside and foot, once to turn the inside, and a final mounting to finish the foot. In the early days many of the bowls were never really finished on the foot. Often the foot was covered with felt to hide the holes left over from being mounted on a faceplate for turning at one mounting. It is my opinion that the foot of the bowl should be finished just as well as the rest of the bowl. This can only be done if the bowl is reverse-turned to allow the foot of the bowl to be turned and sanded. Reverse turning removes all traces of how the bowl was held for turning.

Ideally, the reversed bowl should be held so that the foot is fully accessible for turning and sanding. There are several methods of doing this but they all require that something be made or purchased. Here are a few:

1. Most chuck manufacturers have Cole jaws or jumbo jaws. These jaws do not hold the bowl extremely securely, but well enough to turn the foot without a supporting tailstock, **Figure 7-3** on page 70.

2. The Longworth chuck, **Figure 1-6** on page 13, is not commercially available but can be made in most shops. Instructions for making the Longworth chuck can be found at my web site, www.fholder.com/Woodturning/chuck.htm.

3. The donut chuck has a base plate mounted onto a faceplate and a donut-shaped disk bolted to the base plate with the bowl sandwiched in between. Ideally, a groove is cut into the base plate to fit the rim of the bowl and ensure centering it to the axis of rotation. This mounting is secure enough for very large bowls.

Figure 7-21. Duct tape holds this bowl in a jam-fit chuck so its foot can be turned

4. The vacuum chuck uses a vacuum source to hold the bowl against a disk with a foam facing or a cup with a foam rim mounted on the lathe spindle. Earlier forms used a shop vacuum as the vacuum source. There are now a number of purpose-built vacuum pumps available, as well as disks and cups and methods of attaching the vacuum to the lathe spindle. This method is ideal; it is, however, expensive. See **Figure 1-7**, on page 14.

5. A dome shape mounted onto a faceplate with some form of padding to protect the interior of the bowl can be used on the drive side, with the tailstock used to press the bowl against the dome. This method works very well, but the

foot can never be fully clear for final turning.

6. The jam-fit chuck is the easiest and least expensive method of reversing the bowl for turning the foot. A flat wooden disk is mounted onto a faceplate and trued up. A groove is cut into the disk that will grip the bowl rim. The tailstock is then used to support the bowl for most of the final turning and then backed away so that the very center of the foot can be turned. Duct tape can be used to secure the bowl when the tailstock is backed away, **Figure 7-21.**

It is normal to turn the foot so that a narrow ring of wood actually sets on the table. The center of the foot is generally recessed with turned detailing or other embellishment.

A new product called the rim chuck is designed to hold a bowl while turning the foot to the same quality as the rest of the piece. There are many methods for doing this, but none are as positive as the rim chuck. I reviewed the device in the May 2007 issue of *More Woodturning* and found that, although it is similar in design to the Longworth chuck, it has some significant improvements, and you can purchase it ready to go without having to make it yourself.

I found this chuck useful for holding the rough turned, dried, and warped bowl while truing up the foot for the chuck, see **Figure 7-23.** Without it, I had to jam this rough bowl against the chuck jaws and use a center in the tailstock to approximate the center of rotation. The rim chuck held the rough-turned bowl firmly while I trued up the foot. I then used the rim chuck again to hold the bowl while turning and finishing the foot to the same quality as the rest of the piece. Note: I have used the tailstock for support whenever possible to assist this chuck in holding the bowl. This operation is illustrated in **Figure 7-24.**

Figure 7-22. The turned foot, signed and dated.

Figure 7-23. The rim chuck holds a rough-turned bowl so the foot can be trued.

Figure 7-24. The tailstock helps support the finished bowl while turning the foot.

FAQ 8

Spheres

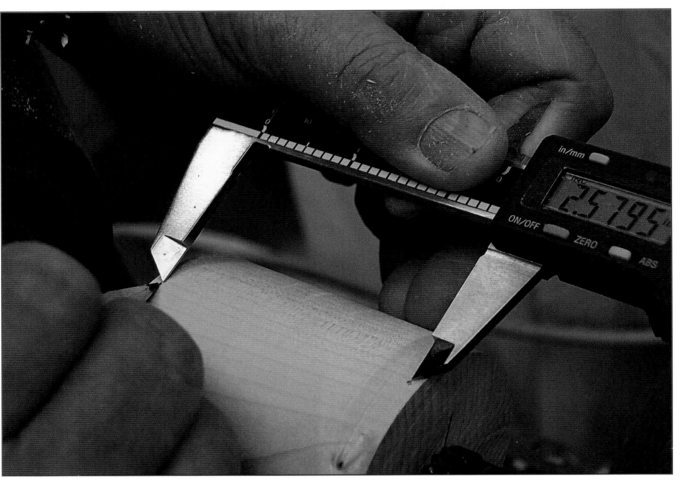

Figure 8-1. To make the blank for a sphere, turn a smooth cylinder and then mark its diameter along its length using calipers.

Q How do I turn a sphere?

There are several ways to turn a sphere: freehand between centers with multiple 90 degree shifts, freehand with a template, freehand using a ring to determine roundness, using a sphere-turning rig, and finally, the most accurate, the traditional billiard ball method. The first method mentioned is perhaps the easiest, however, it is difficult to turn a sphere of a specific size using this method. The traditional billiard ball method is by far the most accurate method for both roundness and for size control.

Q How do I turn a sphere freehand between centers?

I was first introduced to the fun project of making spheres by a Christian Burchard demonstration almost 10 years ago. Christian made all of his spheres between centers and that is the method described in the following section.

Start with a piece of wood mounted between centers in a conventional spindle mounting, that is, with the grain is parallel to the axis of lathe rotation. Use the gouge to make it round and the skew to make it smooth. When satisfied with the surface of the cylinder, measure the diameter with a caliper.

Using the caliper as a measuring device, make marks to indicate the width of the cylinder that will become the sphere, **Figure 8-1**. Lay out a center line between the two outside marks. Holding the pencil on each of the marks in turn, rotate the piece and make the mark all of the way around. At this point, the center (equator) of the sphere and the north and south poles are defined, see **Figure 8-2**. Now, measure half way between the center line and the outside line on each side of the center and make another line all around, **Figure 8-3**. Mark the dimension between the two outside lines on the parting tool and part to that depth outside of each end line, **Figure 8-4**. The sphere blank at this point in shown in **Figure 8-5**.

With the skew or gouge, cut the wood down in a nice slope from the line marking the middle of half of the sphere blank to the bottom of

Figure 8-2. Mark the center line of the sphere on the cylinder.

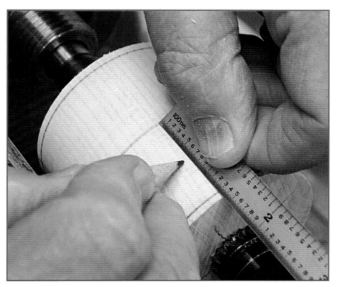

Figure 8-3. Lay out lines marking a point half-way between the center and the outside edge of the sphere.

Figure 8-4. Make a line on the parting tool to mark the depth of the first cut on each end of the sphere blank.

Figure 8-5. Part to the marked depth on each side of the sphere blank.

Figure 8-6. Mount the blank between centers to begin turning the sphere, Make the first cuts on each end at about 45 degrees.

Figure 8-7. A hollowed wood block mounted in a chuck can be used to hold the sphere for further turning.

the parting cut. This gives a slope of about 45 degrees on each end of the sphere. Now, deepen the parting cut on each end until you have a tenon on each end of the sphere blank, just enough to hold the spindle for turning. The blank at this point is shown in **Figure 8-6**. Then, begin to round over each end of the sphere, cutting the end part deeper as the work progresses down each side. Take the tenon on each end down to about 1/2 inch (12mm) in diameter. Maintain the center line throughout this phase of the turning. If the center line is accidentally cut off, make a new one before parting off the tenons.

Use a small faceplate or chuck with a piece of

wood mounted with end grain along the axis of the lathe. Turn it round and then true up the end before hollowing it slightly. Only the edges of the hollow will contact the sphere so make sure that the hollow is deep enough, **Figure 8-7**. For the tailstock end, a live center with a piece of wood fitted to it will work. Mount the sphere between these two points with the center line at the center on each end. That center line is now aligned with the axis of the lathe, that is, you have rotated the sphere 90 degrees for this step, **Figure 8-8**.

Turn on the lathe. The sphere is visibly rotating with a shadow where the high points are located. Use a gouge to cut away the shadow.

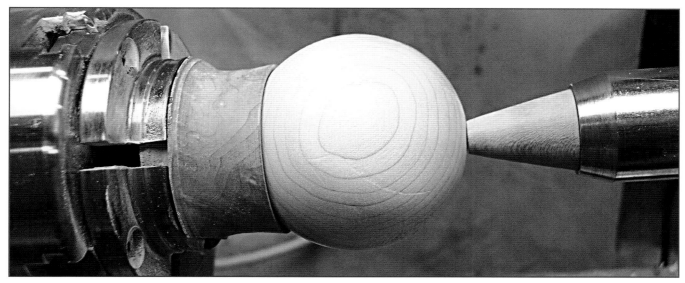

Figure 8-8. The sphere is mounted between the wooden cup in the headstock and a smaller wooden block on the live center. Note that the previous center line is now in line with the axis of rotation and centered on the wooden blocks.

When the sphere is reasonably round, that is, the shadow has diminished, make another center mark. This doesn't have to be perfect center, simply eyeball it and mark with a pencil while the lathe is rotating.

Loosen the tailstock and rotate the sphere 90 degrees to make the new center line along the axis of the lathe. Repeat the process of cutting away the shadow. Keep doing this operation over and over, until the sphere is reasonably round. A scraper can then come into play.

Christian used a shear scraper. I've found that a flat scraper works well. However, a scraper made from an old hole saw with the teeth ground off works best. Ray Key describes the use of such a scraper in making spheres in one of his books. This tubular scraper needs to be smaller than the diameter of the sphere, but as large as possible for best results. In one of his articles in *Woodturning* magazine, Bill Jones mentions using a section of bicycle handlebar for a certain size sphere. Anyway, regardless of what you use to make this tubular scraper from, it must be ground on a disk sander to create a burr on the inside. I believe Ray Key recommends chucking the piece on the lathe and using the tailstock to force a piece of broken

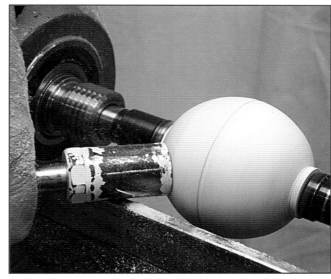

Figure 8-9. A spherical scraper can be made from an old hole saw with the teeth ground off.

grindstone against the end to create this burr. This type of scraper helps to make the sphere round, see **Figure 8-9**.

It is now time to begin sanding on the lathe. However, as you sand, the sphere becomes less round because end grain and side grain cut differently with the sandpaper. Sanding is done just like turning. Sand, rotate 90 degrees, sand, change grit, sand, rotate 90 degrees, sand, change grit, until it is smooth. At this point, wax the sphere and then rub it.

Q What about turning a sphere freehand and using a template?

I often use a set of templates cut out of cardboard to help maintain the size of the ball and to check the roundness of the sphere. Simply draw a circle of the diameter sphere desired on a piece of tablet back, cut it in half, and then cut on the line on each half. Shorten the legs on one of the pieces. The full-half can be used for sizing the diameter of the cylinder and marking its length. Use the other piece for checking the shape as you turn the sphere, **Figure 8-10**. When finished, cut off the small tenons and either finish between centers in cup chucks or simply, as a friend of mine does, grind away the tenon with a disk sander to fit the spherical profile, again checked by the template. That friend also made a circular tool rest that helped him shape the sphere. He was making many spheres for a local club.

Making up a sphere scraper, as described above, is very useful with this method of making spheres. A sphere scraper is a piece of pipe or similar material that is ground flat on the end so that there is a burr on the inside of the pipe. The inside diameter of the pipe should be less than the diameter of the finished sphere. Place it over the tool rest and in contact with the surface of the sphere. The scraper helps to true up the sphere into a good spherical form.

Figure 8-10. Check the roundness of the sphere with a template.

Figure 8-11. Check for roundness using a ring. This ring was made from a slice of PVC pipe.

Q What about using a ring to check for roundness?

This is another technique that I've seen used to determine roundness. In this method, use a turned ring or a slice off of a piece of PVC pipe with a very flat surface. You can use this as a gauge to determine where wood needs to be removed, **Figure 8-11**. It seems to work very well to help to round the surface of the sphere, but does nothing concerning sizing.

Q What about the sphere-turning rig?

My first sphere-turning rig was made of wood after the one described in *Woodturning Wizardry* by David Springett. It worked well, but being made from wood, it had a certain amount of flex. I found that an all-metal rig is available from Craft Supplies Ltd. in the UK. This rig fits into the tool post hole of the lathe banjo and the point of rotation must be precisely under the sphere. With everything set up properly, this rig works great. Unfortunately, it is almost impossible to get the tool rest hole exactly aligned to center under the sphere. I finally solved the problem by making a separate base for the rig from pipe fittings. A wooden base was attached to the pipe flange with a spacer piece to fit between the lathe bed bars. This automatically centered the rig's pivot point under the lathe's center of rotation. **Figure 8-12** shows my sphere-turning rig.

To turn a sphere with this rig, mount a piece of wood in the lathe and turn it round and to the diameter of the finished sphere, plus a little bit for sanding. Then with calipers, measure the diameter of the cylinder and lay out that dimension on the cylinder with a pencil. Make parting cuts on the outside edges of the pencil marks down to about one inch diameter and use a gouge to cut away the excess. The result will be a cylinder that is as long as it is across. This is the sphere blank. Now remove the tool rest from the lathe and install the sphere-turning rig. Adjust the tool extension so that it just cuts off each corner of the blank as you swing the tool to the right and to the left. Then, through many tool extension adjustments, bring the wood down to a spherical shape. Your center line should just remain on the blank.

Next remove the sphere-turning rig and replace the tool rest assembly. Using a 3/8-inch (10mm) spindle gouge, reduce the extensions to a thin section, you are much less likely to cut in too deep this way. A handsaw or parting tool then quickly finishes the job.

Figure 8-12. This photo shows the author's sphere turning rig. The basic tool is available from Craft Supplies Ltd. in England. The mounting base is made from pipe fittings. The cutting tool is a bedan.

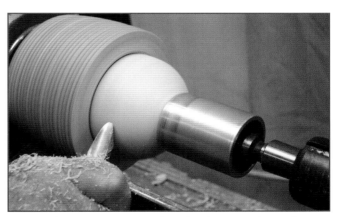

Figure 8-13. Turn away the shadow on the sphere mounted between a jam-fit chuck and a tail center.

Remount the sphere on the lathe with a cup-shaped piece mounted on the headstock spindle and a cup-shaped piece mounted on the live tailstock center. Then, as described previously, turn away the shadow and sand to finish, **Figure 8-13.**

Q What is the traditional billiard ball method?

Figure 8-14. Align the center points to be parallel to the face of a faceplate or perpendicular to the axis of rotation.

Figure 8-15. To turn billiard balls, cut a groove to the precise diameter using a parting tool and a set of spring calipers.

One final freehand method, the one used for many years to turn billiard balls, is to rough-turn the sphere freehand, perhaps using a template to check the work. Then rotate it 90 degrees and mount it into a jam-fit chuck, making sure that the two center points are exactly on a line parallel to a faceplate or perpendicular to the axis of rotation, **Figure 8-14.** This can be checked with a pencil mark. When it is exactly positioned, use a caliper and a parting tool to cut a groove to the exact desired size, **Figure 8-15.**

Again, rotate the sphere 90 degrees and mount it into the jam-fit chuck. Now, turn away the sphere surface until the groove just disappears, **Figure 8-16.** Reverse and repeat for the other half-sphere and you have a near perfectly round sphere at a specified diameter. I find that this method works extremely well when you need precisely dimensioned spheres that are as near round as you can make them. I've used this method to make the 2-1/2 inch (64mm) spheres

Figure 8-16. Turn part of the material away until the groove disappears. The groove is still visible on the unturned area of the sphere.

that I need for my Chinese Balls. I believe they are more perfect than any of the other methods that I've used. There's more work featuring spheres on page 87.

Figure 8-17. Fred Holder, Chinese Ball.

Figure 8-18. Malcolm Tibbets, Pearls from the Forest.

Figure 8-19. Christian Delorn, of France.

FAQ 9

Hollow Vessels

Figure 9-1. Hollow form by Art Liestiman.

Q How do I turn a hollow form?

Hollow forms are generally taller than they are wide and are therefore normally turned from log sections with the grain running from the base to top or parallel to the axis of rotation. As a result, the hollowing is into the end grain, **Figure 9-1**, which requires different tools than when hollowing bowls where the grain is perpendicular to the axis of rotation. The end grain hollowing tools available are mostly scraper type tools with small tips. Cutting type tools can be used if the cut is made from the center of the opening toward the outside. This is where a hook tool comes into its own because it is designed to do that type of cutting. This is true also of ring tools such as the Oneway Termite. There are also several tools on the market that use ring-type cutters with guards over the ring to help limit the amount of cut the tool makes. One of these tools is the Proforme Tool from Woodcut Tools of New Zealand.

Figure 9-2 illustrates a number of end-grain hollowing tools. All of them work. The key for good cutting control is that no more than 20 percent of a tool's length should extend over the tool rest into the workpiece. Many of these tools, therefore, are limited to the depth to which they can be used because of their overall length. For first hollowing tools, it is a good idea to select tools that have a flat on the bottom to help reduce rotational forces on the tool.

If you have internet access, Lyn J. Mangiameli wrote an excellent five-part series on hollowing tools that was published in *More Woodturning* beginning in the July 2004 issue and ending in the December 2004 issue. These articles can be found at my web site, www.fholder.com. If you are just getting into doing hollow forms and wish some detailed guidance on purchasing tools, this is about the most extensive treatment of the subject that I've read anywhere.

Because hollowing vessels can be hard on the anatomy, the stabilized boring bar came into

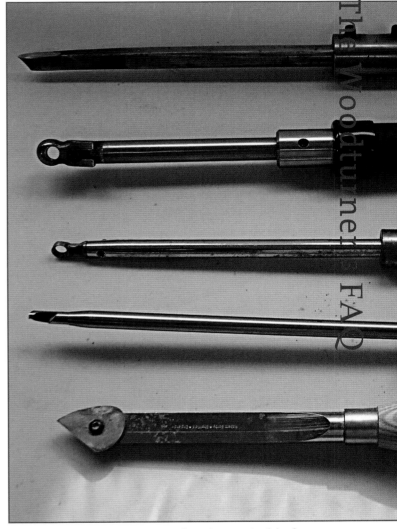

Figure 9-2. This selection of tools is suitable for hollow forms (from the top): Kelton hollower, Hamlet hollowing tool, Oneway Termite ring tool, Berger tool, and Robert Sorby multi-tip hollowing tool.

existence. I'm not sure who came up with this idea, but I first saw it used by Lyle Jamieson and later by Frank Sudol. In 1999, I wrote a report on a further development that made hollowing vessels even easier: the laser pointer used to measure wall thickness during the hollowing. This system, with some form of stabilized boring bar, has enabled many people to make hollow forms that they would never have attempted with standard hollowing tools.

Q How do I turn hollow vessels with standard tools?

You begin with mounting the wood into a chuck or onto a faceplate. I believe that most hollow-form turners prefer the faceplate mount with many very long screws. Unfortunately, screws do not hold very well when screwed into end grain. Wally Dickerman, a very experienced hollow-vessel turner who lives in Arizona, showed his method in a demonstration to my local club several years ago. Wally drills holes into the side of the log and glues in sections of hardwood dowels. These are located so that his faceplate screws will pass through the dowels. This provides side grain to hold the screw threads and works very well.

I personally prefer a chuck with at least a four-inch diameter jaw, with the jaws compressing onto a 4-inch (100mm) diameter tenon and a good stout shoulder for the jaws to butt against. With the chuck fitted properly to the tenon, this set-up has tremendous holding power.

Once the wood is mounted securely on the lathe spindle, turn the outside to the near finished shape of the vessel. You need something to gauge the inside of the vessel against. The reason I say near the finished shape is that you do not want to turn the base of the vessel too small until after it has been hollowed. You do want most of the vessel to be very near final shape to use in measuring wall thickness.

With the outside shape determined and the end of the blank faced off, drill a hole down the center of the piece to very near final depth of the inside. Since end grain likes to be cut from the center toward the outside, the hole makes a good starting point for a cut. On your first few pieces, don't make the opening too small. It is easier to manipulate your tools through a larger opening. Remember, you are turning blind, that is, you can't see the tip of your tool except in the very beginning. Work your way toward the bottom in steps. First enlarge the hole to about the diameter of the opening all of the way to the bottom. Then working down into the vessel,

Figure 9-3. A steady rest helps stabilize the hollow vessel while you turn the interior.

enlarge the hole all of the way to the inside wall dimension. Try to avoid leaving ridges or valleys and check the wall thickness often.

If the vessel is very tall, it is a good idea to set up a steady rest to help stabilize the vessel during the hollowing process, as shown in **Figure 9-3**. Several companies manufacture good steady rests, or you can make your own from some plywood and roller blade wheels.

After the inside shape has been well hollowed, I prefer to shift to one of the round or teardrop shape scraper type tools to make smoothing the inside much easier. The deeper you go, the longer your tool must be. Remember, no more than 20 percent of the tool length should extend over the tool rest. As the amount of extension goes up, the diameter of the shaft must also increase to eliminate tool vibration.

When the inside hollowing is done, the outside may be final-turned, sanded, and a finish applied. Many turners do not sand the inside further down than what they can reach with their finger. However, a vessel is much nicer if the inside is sanded as well as the outside. The vessel is then reversed and the bottom finished.

Q How can I hold the vessel to final-turn the bottom?

The best method that I've encountered for final-turning the bottom of a hollow vessel is a jig that the San Diego Woodturners had made up back in 2002. I purchased one of these and found it invaluable when remounting a hollow vessel to turn the foot. Oskar Kirsten designed the jig and Nan Bushley made design improvements before the club had any units manufactured.

Figure 9-4. This tool, for mounting hollow forms on the lathe, was developed and marketed by the San Diego Woodturners Club.

The jig is a long steel rod about 3/4 inch (20mm) in diameter. One end of it has a Morse taper #2 machined onto it. The other end has a 1/4-inch (6mm) hole bored into it for gluing in a 1-inch (25mm) sanding mandrel. On the rod, there is a plastic cone with a pair of set-screws. The cone slides up and down the shaft except when the set-screws are tightened. This jig is shown in **Figure 9-4**.

When you are ready to reverse-turn the foot of a hollow form, you mount the jig into the spindle taper. Next you place your hollow form over the rod until the rod touches the bottom of the vessel. The sanding mandrel with a sanding disk presses onto the inside bottom of the vessel. The tailstock presses the other side of the bottom. The cone is then slid up the shaft until the pointed end of the cone engages the mouth of the vessel. The set-screws are then tightened. You are ready to turn the foot. The advantages of this jig are that the piece is driven at the foot instead of through the body of the vessel. **Figure 9-5** shows a hollow vessel set up on this jig.

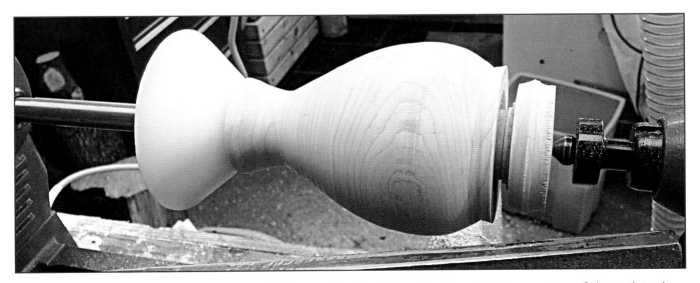

Figure 9-5. This vase has been mounted between the San Diego tool and the live center of the tailstock. Now the foot can be finish-turned to leave only a very tiny stem, which can be removed with a knife or sharp gouge.

Q What is a stabilized boring bar and how it is used?

A stabilized boring bar such as that produced by Lyle Jamieson uses a secondary tool rest to support a D-shaped section of rod. This tool rest captures the D section and keeps it from rotating, but is rather wide to enable the tool to be maneuvered as needed during the hollowing process. One end of the D is fitted with a socket to accept 3/4-inch (19mm) shaft hollowing tools. The shaft of the hollowing tool rests on the lathe tool rest. This arrangement enables one to hollow vessels with minimum stress on the operator. The Jamieson system is shown in **Figure 9-6**.

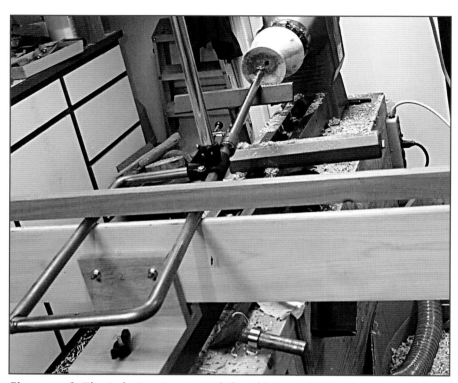

Figure 9-6. The Lyle Jamieson stabilized boring bar has an extension that slides in the wooden gate.

There are several other stabilized hollowing rigs being manufactured that work in the same general way. The Kelton hollowing rig manufactured in New Zealand was my first of these stabilized units. It is heavy and rugged and uses three bars arranged in a triangular fashion that are mounted to another bar on the secondary tool rest. The unit then uses the Kelton hollowing tools for the actual hollowing. The hollowing tools ride on the lathe's tool rest.

I have two other stabilized hollowing rigs

manufactured by Turningways, which use a circular bar that rides in a slot in the secondary tool rest and keeps the tool from rotating. It comes in two sizes. Their Min-O-Bar hollowing system (**Figure 9-7**) is my favorite for smaller hollow forms. It works extremely well, as does its big brother, shown in **Figure 1-1** on page 10, which is made larger and of heavier stock.

Each of these devices is available with a laser pointer to help judge the wall thickness of the hollow form as it is being turned.

Q How can you use a laser pointer to judge wall thickness?

In June 1999, Dave Thompson of Seattle, Washington, attended the American Association of Woodturners Symposium in Tacoma, Washington, and watched Frank Sudol hollowing large, thin-walled vessels using a light attached to his cutting tool. Frank judged wall thickness by how much light showed through the wall of the vessel. Frank could only make this work on light colored wet wood. Dave thought, if you can use a light on the inside of a vessel to judge wall thickness, why not use a light on the outside? Of course, you would need a very condensed light beam that is no larger than the tip of your cutting tool. Enter the laser pointer. The laser pointer has a very condensed beam of red light and seemed to offer what Dave needed.

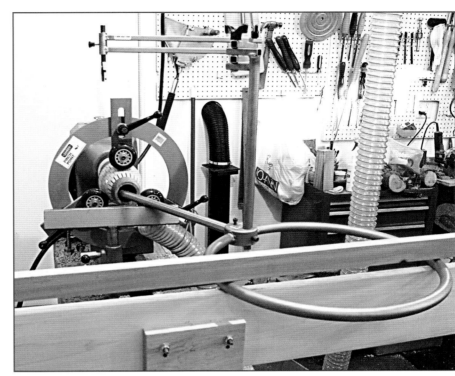

Figure 9-7. The Min-O-Bar hollowing system with the Articulaser, manufactured and distributed by Turningways, is being used to hollow a small vase.

Dave reasoned that if you mounted the laser pointer above the work but pointed onto the very edge of the cutter, and if you could keep your tool level so that the pointer would hit the workpiece on the outside to indicate where the cutter was on the inside, you would know where your cutter was inside the hollow vessel. The boring bar that Dave built provided the stability needed, and the laser pointer provided the light beam.

Dave asked me to write this up and publish it in *More Woodturning*, which I did in the December 1999 issue. Once this story was published, all of the people working with stabilized boring bars immediately adopted it and made up laser-holding fixtures for their boring bars. Originally, Dave adjusted the laser pointer to hit exactly on the tip of his cutter so that he knew exactly where the cutter was inside the vessel. Subsequent users are shifting the light beam to the side of the cutting tip by the amount of wall thickness desired. Thus, when the light drops off the side of the vessel, you are at the desired wall thickness. Using this approach requires you to reposition the laser beam as you cut down into the vessel to make sure the spacing between the cutter and light is at the right point on the cutter. Turningways came up with the Articulaser which can be used on their boring bars or adapted to other boring bars. The Min-O-Bar hollowing system with the Articulaser is shown in **Figure 9-7**.

FAQ 10

Small Projects

Figure 10-1. This selection of wine bottle stoppers was made by the author.

Q What are some small projects that I might turn?

Small projects can be turned on any lathe, but are best suited for the mini-lathes on the market today. A wine bottle stopper is an especially useful project that takes very little time to do and produces a beautiful and useful item to use in your home, to give to a friend, or to sell at a craft fair. Writing pens are also useful items and do well at craft fairs. The spinner top is an especially suitable item for children from 3 to 93. Light pulls are useful in areas where overhead lights are operated with a pull chain. In England, they are mandatory in bathrooms. Needle cases make a nice receptacle for storing sewing needles. Finally, the Christmas tree ornament made from wood is a very nice addition to your tree.

Q How do I turn a wine bottle stopper?

When I began making bottle stoppers, **Figure 10-1**, cork stoppers were all that was available. On my first dozen stoppers, I drilled the hole through the cork using a board with a tapered hole, a drill press, and a 3/8-inch (10mm) Forstner bit. I lost about one out of five corks while drilling and decided to purchase predrilled corks in the future.

There is no specific size requirement for the knob part of the stopper, but if it is too large, it looks out of place on the wine bottle. After making a hundred or so with sizes all over the place, I settled on a blank size of 1-1/4 x 1-1/4 x 2 inches (30mm x 30mm x 50mm). You must exercise care to make sure both ends are parallel so that the hole you drill for the dowel will not be at an angle. Mark an X on one end of the blank and drill a 3/8-inch (10mm) hole about 3/4 inch (19mm) to 1 inch (25mm) deep with a brad-point drill, as shown in **Figure 10-2**. A drill press is nice if you have one, but you can drill them with a hand drill or hold the blank in a chuck and drill the hole on the lathe.

There are a number of ways to hold the blank while turning it, for example, you can use a jam-fit chuck in the dowel hole with the tail center providing pressure to prevent slippage; you can use a screw chuck; you can make up a 3/8-inch (10mm) pin chuck; or you can glue in the dowel (**Figure 10-3**) and hold it with some form of chuck. I found the dowel chuck,

Figure 10-2. Drill the bottle stopper blank on the drill press. To protect your fingers, hold the workpiece in the drill press vise.

Figure 10-3. These bottle stopper blanks have 2-1/2 inch (65mm) dowels glued into the hole.

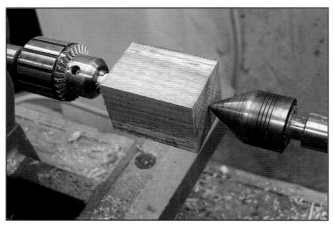

Figure 10-4. To turn the bottle stopper, grip the blank in the jaws of a dowel chuck or collet chuck.

Figure 10-5. Sand the bottle stopper through the grits up to 600 grit.

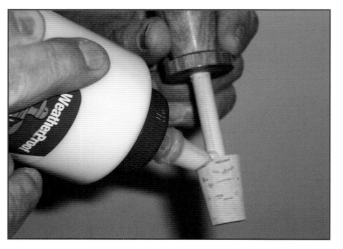

Figure 10-6. Apply the glue to the dowel and the face of the cork. Twist the cork onto the dowel until glue squeezes out.

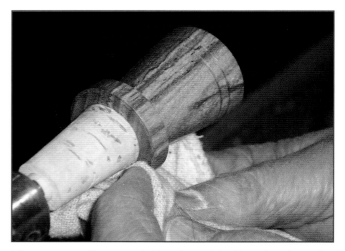

Figure 10-7. Remount the dowel in the chuck and wipe away the squeezed-out glue.

available from Craft Supplies USA in Provo, Utah, to be the best method. I cut my 3/8-inch (10mm) dowels to 2-1/2 inches (65mm) in length and glue them into the hole drilled in the stopper blank with Titebond II glue.

The dowel is inserted into the dowel chuck (see **Figure 10-4**) as far as it will go. The tailstock is then brought up with a live center to help support the workpiece during initial turning and is backed off when you turn the very top of the stopper. I use a skew chisel to true up the end of the blank with the dowel to ensure the cork will have a square seat. The shape of the stopper is a matter of your creative abilities, or you can look at pictures in books to get ideas.

Sand in steps up to 600 grit or higher, **Figure 10-5**, and apply finish. The finish that I used on most of the stoppers that I sold over the years was a sort of French polish mixture of shellac, alcohol, and boiled linseed oil in equal parts. Apply this and let it soak in. Burnish it in with the damp cloth used to apply the mixture, and you have a near French polish finish, **Figure 10-7**.

Remove the stopper from the chuck and slip the predrilled cork onto the end of the dowel about 3/8 inch (10mm), just enough to hold the stopper upright. Apply a little Titebond II glue to the dowel at the join with the cork, **Figure 10-6**. Rotate the cork a couple of times to even up the glue and then screw the cork onto the dowel until it mates with the knob. This spreads glue evenly on the dowel and cork, and spreads glue evenly on the face of the stopper knob.

About 3/8 inch (10mm) of dowel should protrude from the end of the cork, as shown in **Figure 10-7**. Put this into the dowel chuck and spin the stopper to wipe off any glue and then part off the dowel at the end of the cork, see **Figure 10-8**. A light touch on a sanding disk is a nice way to finish the end of the dowel and the cork. Put no finish on the end of the dowel lest you contaminate the wine. **Figure 10-1** on page 94 shows a selection of bottle stoppers.

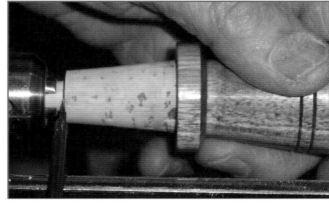

Figure 10-8. Part off the dowel using a thin parting tool. This tool was made from a hardened concrete nail.

Q How do I make a pen?

There is a wide range of mechanical pen kits on the market and a number of books and videos telling how to make them, **Figure 10-9**. I found that pens are mostly assembly work and very little turning. I had enough assembly work when I worked in an aircraft factory many years ago. Thus I only made one pen and pencil set and then crossed them off my list of things to make. Then I saw a pen turned from wood with an insert from a Bic pen. This was a fun pen to make and that is the type of pen described here, **Figure 10-10**.

Figure 10-9. This mechanical pen was made from one of the pen kits.

The pen blank should be about 1/2-inch (12.5mm) square in cross section and slightly longer than the Bic pen that you will be taking the insert from. Mount one end of the blank in the small jaws of a four-jaw scroll chuck (I use a Nova chuck with the 25 mm jaws) and bring up the tailstock with a live center to support the other end of the blank. Turn the blank round with a roughing gouge or a skew chisel. If the blank was 1/2-inch (12.5mm)

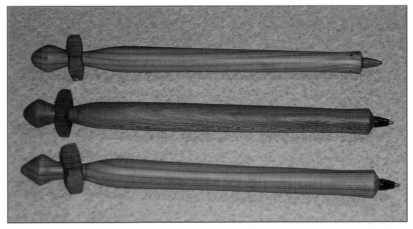

Figure 10-10. These pens were turned from wood and drilled to accept a Bic pen insert. These pens have loose square rings.

square, it should clean up at about 3/8 inch (10mm) in diameter or a little more. Now, back away the tailstock and take a 9/64-inch (4mm) drill that is 6 inches (150mm) long and grip it in a chuck or make a handle for it. Hold the chuck or handle freehand. Align the drill with the bed of the lathe and start drilling in the dimple made by the live center. Drill in about 3/8 inch (10mm) to 1/2 inch (13mm) at a time. Remove the drill completely and clean the flutes before drilling any more. Continue this until the hole is a bit deeper than the Bic pen insert is long.

Bring the tailstock back to support the end of the blank while the pen is turned to finished shape. Mark the end of the hole that you drilled on the outside of the blank. Put any beads or decoration past the end of hole mark. Finish turning the pen, sand, and apply finish. Then, back off the tailstock and enlarge the hole with a 5/32-inch (4.5mm) drill for about 1 inch (25mm). This allows the larger portion of the Bic insert to enter the hole. Part off the pen, sand the very end, and insert the Bic insert. Your pen is complete.

Q How do I turn a spinner top?

My spinner tops are not fancy or ornate, they're just good spinners. That is what is important. I use 3/4 (20mm) inch to 1 inch (25mm) thick slices from limbs that are 1-1/2 inches (35mm) to 2 inches (50mm) in diameter, or scraps from turning other things. I drill a 3/8-inch (10mm) hole as close to center as possible, Figure 10-11, and insert and glue in a section of 3/8-inch (10mm) dowel rod, **Figure 10-11**, that has been cut to 2-1/2 inches (65mm) long. When the glue is dry, about 24 hours, I chuck the dowel up in my dowel chuck that I use to turn bottle stoppers and push the dowel in as far as it

will go while turning the large part of the top, **Figure 10-12**. I make it round and then turn the bottom with a long slope to the point. The cut needs to be made from the rim to the point in one continuous cut, **Figure 10-13**.

When I'm satisfied with the shape of the bottom, I turn the top portion of the top. Over the years, I have found that a top with a recessed upper part (sort of bowl-like) spins best, see **Figure 10-14**. I try to keep the edge under 0.1 inch (2.5mm) and generally shoot for about 0.05 inch (1.25mm) thickness. Then and

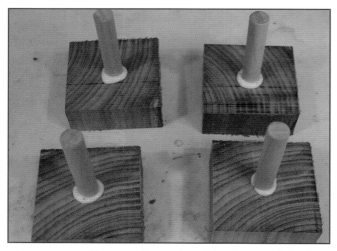

Figure 10-11. These spinner top blanks consist of thin wooden squares with dowel glued into them. The slices of wood work best when the grain runs from top to bottom, so it will be the same as the dowel.

Figure 10-12. Mount the top blank on the lathe in the dowel chuck.

Figure 10-13. Cut the taper on what will be the bottom of the top. This should be one continuous cut from rim to tip.

Figure 10-14. Turn a bowl-shaped recess into the top portion of the spinner, leaving a little shouldered section around the dowel..

Figure 10-15. Turn the stem down to about 1/8 inch (3mm) in diameter.

Figure 10-16. These spinner tops were turned from planks, with 3/8-inch (10mm) dowels for stems.

only then do I pull the dowel out further to turn the stem. I generally turn the stem to 1/8 inch (3mm) or less in diameter, by about 1 inch (25mm) long, **Figure 10-15.**

I then sand the whole thing and apply a coat of wax. The wax brings out the color in the wood and makes the top look better, it's especially effective when people are watching you turn the top. I part off with a skew, leaving the top of the stem with a tapered, but slightly blunt,

point. This way the top can be spun either way, that is, on the stem or on the point. **Figure 10-16** shows some finished spinner tops.

I normally turn my tops with the grain running in the spindle-turning direction (parallel to the axis of the lathe), because when the grain runs the other direction the wood is likely to chip out where it joins the dowel on the bottom. It really doesn't hurt the top, other than its looks, and that bothers me.

Q How do I turn a light pull?

Figure 10-17. This completed light pull, by Martin Pidgen, is ready to be removed from the lathe.

Figure 10-18. This dowel, mounted in a dowel chuck, has a 5/16-inch (8mm) tenon on its end.

Figure 10-19. Drill the 9/64-inch (4mm) hole all the way through the light-pull blank.

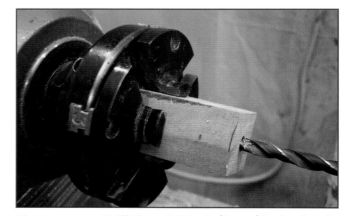

Figure 10-20. Drill the 5/16 inch (8mm) hole about 1/2 inch (12mm) into the light pull blank.

Martin Pidgen, a production turner in England, markets his work through more than 40 galleries. Martin is, perhaps, best known for his light pulls. In England the household current is 220 volts, and the electrical code says that every light in a bathroom must have a pull cord to help prevent shocks. Martin has cornered the market on these. He has made about 175,000 of his plain pulls and about 75,000 of his acorn pulls, which are made of boxwood and oak. He actually makes pulls out of 100 different types of wood. **Figure 10-17** shows one of Martin's light pulls nearing completion.

Martin begins a light pull by mounting a dowel chuck in the headstock and fitting a 3/8 inch (10mm) dowel to the chuck. He turns a step on the end of this dowel, as shown in **Figure 10-18.** This becomes the drive tool for his light pull. The wood is then predrilled with a 9/64-inch (4mm) hole all of the way through, **Figure 10-19,** and then a 5/16-inch (8mm) hole about 1/2-inch (12mm) deep, **Figure 10-20,** in what will become the bottom of the pull. The 3/8-inch (10mm) dowel is turned to fit the 5/16-inch (8mm) hole and becomes the jam-fit chuck for turning the pull. The tailstock with a live center supports the other end and applies pressure to the drive end.

Martin uses a gouge to turn the wood round and then to shape. He can turn about six per hour. He prepares the wood, cuts it to size and predrills it, and places it on the shelf. When he gets an order, he turns the pieces. This way he always has dry wood to work with.

Q How do I turn a needle case?

Needle cases are made from hardwood that is about 3/4 to 1 inch (20 to 25mm) square and about 5 inches (125mm) long. I mount one end of the wood in a Nova chuck with the 1 inch (25mm) jaws, and carefully position it so that about 1 inch of the stock is held in the chuck. Turn about 1/2 inch (12mm) on the end round, as shown in **Figure 10-21**. This will later be used to chuck the body of the needle case. Part off the body of the needle case, leaving about one inch of stock in the chuck. With a Jacob's chuck in the tailstock, drill a 3/8-inch (10mm) hole about 1/2-inch (12mm) deep in the piece remaining in the chuck, **Figure 10-22**. Clean up the face of the piece, then remove it from the chuck and set it aside. This will be the top of the needle case.

Mount the tenon that was turned on the long piece in the chuck and drill a 1/4-inch (6mm) hole about the length of the drill bit, being careful not to drill too deep, **Figure 10-23**. Mark the bottom of the hole on the outside of the workpiece, then move down about 1/4 inch (6mm) and make a parting cut in about 1/8 inch (3mm) to mark the bottom. Turn a tenon on the end to snugly fit into the short piece's 3/8-inch (10mm) hole, see **Figure 10-24**. If it is a little bit loose, you may be able to tighten it up with a little moisture, spit works quite well.

Now bring up the tailstock to help support the short piece, **Figure 10-25**. Turn the top from the short piece, don't try to finish the finial on top

Figure 10-21. Mount the blank in the dowel chuck and turn a tenon on the end for remounting.

Figure 10-22. Drill a 3/8-inch (10mm) hole in the piece that will become the top of the needle case.

Figure 10-23. Drill a 1/4-inch (6mm) hole in the bottom part of the needle case.

Figure 10-24. Turn a tenon on the piece mounted in the chuck to fit the hole in the top piece.

Figure 10-25. Mount the top portion on the base and hold it with the live center so the entire needle case can be turned together.

Figure 10-26. After turning the body and the lid together, back off the tailstock so that the very top of the lid can be turned to its final shape.

at this time. Turn the bottom of the needle case to some pleasing shape and to blend with the top. When satisfied with the shape, back off the tailstock and final-turn the finial on the top (**Figure 10-26**). Now it is just a matter of sanding and finishing.

I use my bottle-stopper finish on these: 1/3 prepared shellac, 1/3 alcohol, and 1/3 boiled linseed oil by volume. Shake well before applying. Take a little on a rag and saturate the surface. Then turn on the lathe and buff with a dry part of the rag, then come back with the

damp part of the rag and buff some more. If it's not shiny enough, apply more solution and repeat the buffing until you are satisfied.

Incidentally, any four-jaw chuck will work that can clamp down on these sizes. If you don't have a chuck, you can use faceplates with waste blocks attached and glue the pieces to the waste block with Yellow Label Hot Stuff cyanoacrylate glue. It is always a good idea to turn a shallow recess in the waste block to help center the workpiece. A completed needle case is shown in **Figure 10-27**.

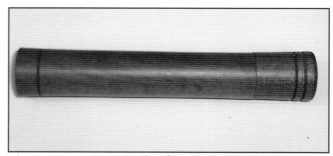

Figure 10-27. Here is the finished needle case.

Q How do I turn a Christmas ornament?

The turned Christmas ornament is made in many forms. The traditional ball-shaped form with an icicle is the type most woodturners make. However, bells, birdhouses, and a wide range of other shaped ornaments are also turned. **Figure 10-28** shows one of my ornaments.

My ornaments generally have a ball as their main feature. If you don't want to turn balls, but like the ornaments with the ball component, you can buy balls that are factory-turned, and simply hollow them and add an icicle and top finial to make a very respectable ornament.

Many turners make ornaments with a squashed ball shape that is much larger in diameter than it is high. The icicle is generally longer on these, to make up for the reduction in the height of the ball.

Laminations of decorative woods are often used in the making of ornaments. Also, some turners use the inside-out form of construction where four pieces are glued together with paper in between the glue joints and some shape is turned in the wood, **Figure 10-30** (next page). The pieces are pried apart, rotated 180 degrees, and glued back together to make up a hollow object with shaped windows to the outside, **Figure 10-31**. This object is then turned into shape, **Figure 10-32**. An icicle and finial may be added to produce a very attractive and unusual ornament.

Another ornament form is the bird house ornament. My birdhouses are generally made using a three-piece construction with the top and bottom from a contrasting color wood. I personally like the lighter wood for the hollow main part of the house with darker wood for the top and bottom.

I recount all of this to illustrate that the making of ornaments is really an individual thing and

Figure 10-28. Christmas ornaments typically have a central ball with a rounded top finial and a long spike.

that what you produce is limited only by your own imagination. How you construct the ball (round, squashed, elongated) and how long you make the finial and icicle are pretty much a matter of personal choice, or what looks good.

Unless you are already proficient at making balls, or as some people like to call them "spherical shapes", you will find that making the ball and hollowing it to be the most difficult part. Many people use a homemade tool with an Allen wrench as the metal part, adding a handle and grinding a cutting edge on the short leg of the Allen wrench. This makes a very inexpensive hollowing tool that works great for doing Christmas ornaments.

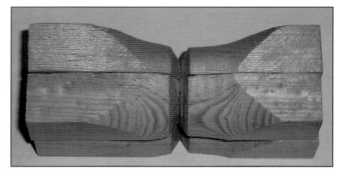

Figure 10-30. To make an inside-out turning, glue four pieces of wood together and turn the outside shape.

Figure 10-31. Reverse the four pieces and glue them together to put the turned part inside and to create a small window in the glued-up blank.

Figure 10-32. Finish-turn the outside of the blank to complete the inside-out turning.

Figure 10-29. Birdhouse ornament.

Figure 10-33. Birdhouse Christmas ornaments by Joe Aquila.

Figure 10-34. Birdhouse ornament by Dale Nish.

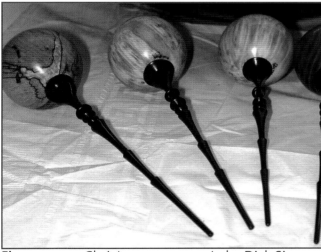

Figure 10-35. Christmas ornaments by Dick Sing.

FAQ 11

Decorative Effects

Figure 11-1. This Stephen Hatcher platter that has been carved and filled with crushed rock inlay.

Q How do I enhance my turnings?

Whenever one goes to a large symposium such as the Utah Woodturning Symposium in Provo, Utah, or the American Association of Woodturners annual symposium, the Instant Gallery is filled with beautifully turned objects with more and more of them being enhanced in some manner. The processes used include carving, various forms of texturing such as chatter work, the Robert Sorby texturing tool or even a hand-held power tool such as the Dremel. Pyrography, and coloring are also used.

Q How can one enhance a turning by carving?

Figure 11-2. This piece by Andi Wolfe was turned and then carved and colored.

Figure 11-3. Guilio Marcolongo of Australia made this fancy box with carved feet.

There are a great many carving tools available that can be used to carve part of a turned object to make it into an entirely different piece of art. There are hand-held electrical tools suitable for smaller types of carving and the four-inch right angle grinders that are used with cutting blades similar to those of a chain saw that can be used for more extensive carving, especially on a larger piece. Stephen Hatcher and Andi Wolfe are two woodturning artists who do carving on most, if not all, of their turnings. **Figure 11-1** shows a Stephen Hatcher platter that has been carved and then filled with crushed rock inlay. **Figure 11-2** is one of Andi Wolfe's turned, carved, and colored vessels. One of the most common forms of carving for bowls, boxes, and hollow forms is the carving of feet for the object. This is often done using round files and rasps, but can also be done with power tools. **Figure 11-3** shows a fancy box with carved feet done by Guilio Marcolongo of Australia.

Q How can I texture my work?

Texturing is a process whereby a beautifully smoothed surface is then made rough by some means. Chatter is one of the common methods used and is especially useful on end grain surfaces. The Robert Sorby texturing tool allows one to chose different texture patterns by varying the angle of application of the tool to the rotating wood. Another common method is to use some small high-speed tool with a ball-shaped cutter to texture a surface. Another method sometimes uses a wire brush mounted on a hand-held right-angle grinder to texture the surface.

Q What is a chatter tool and how can I use it?

One of the most common methods of applying chatter is with the use of a chatter tool, which is a thin-bladed cutter mounted in a handle, **Figure 11-4**. When the tool is applied to the rotating wood it tends to vibrate and creates a chattered pattern on the smooth surface, **Figure 11-5**. This type of tool is most effectively used on end-grain surfaces such as the top of end-grain boxes and, as Bonnie Klein has so aptly shown, on spinner tops.

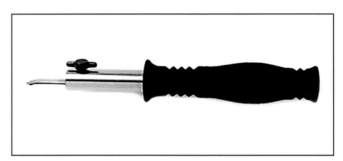

Figure 11-4. A chatter tool has a thin blade that vibrates as it cuts.

One other form of chatter, though it is less controlled, is obtained by pressing too hard when cutting on a flexible object. This is often obtained on spindle turned work when it is not desirable. However, it can be used to good effect in some instances. Michael Hosaluk is noted for doing this on his spinner tops.

Figure 11-5. These tops with chatter patterns were colored with felt-tip pens.

Q What is a Robert Sorby texturing tool?

Several years ago, Robert Sorby of Sheffield, England, introduced their texturing tool, which is a multi-pointed wheel mounted on the end of a round shaft that is fitted with a handle, **Figure 11-6**. The multi-pointed wheel rotates when it is applied to the rotating wood and creates different patterns of texture depending upon the angle of application. One of the simplest patterns, and my favorite, is an orange peel effect, which is a pattern of indentations on the surface that

Figure 11-6. The Robert Sorby texturing and spiraling tool has a multi-point cutting wheel.

gives the appearance of orange peel. By simply changing the angle at which the wheel engages the wood, the pattern can be changed.

Q How can I use a Dremel type tool to texture?

When one of the small high-speed tools such as the Dremel are fitted with a small ball-shaped cutter, they can be used most effectively to apply a controlled texture to the smooth surface of an object. This method requires more skill and practice than some of the other methods of texturing, but can produce very striking types of texture in the hands of a skilled artist such as Michael Hosaluk, **Figure 11-7**.

Figure 11-7. Michael Hosaluk, Squirmy Box.

Q How can I make flutes and spirals on my turned objects?

Both flutes and spirals can be cut by hand with carving chisels or with powered hand-held tools. The router can also be used to cut flutes and spirals. Normally the router method is used on such projects such as chair legs and railing spindles, which really do have to match one another.

Q How can I cut spirals by hand?

Hand-cut spirals (actually, helices) must be laid out by first drawing a number of equally spaced parallel lines on the turning surface, **Figure 11-8**. This can be done using the indexing head on the lathe headstock, with the tool rest. Then a number of equally spaced circumference lines are drawn between the two areas where the spirals will traverse. This creates a number of equal-sized rectangles on the surface of the object on which the spirals are to be applied. Now, picking a starting point at one end of the layout, draw a diagonal line across the first rectangle, as shown in **Figure 11-9**. Rotate the turning a bit and continue the diagonal line across the next rectangle. Repeat this operation until the line reaches the opposite end of the area to be spiraled.

This layout has given you one spiral around the object. You may shift one or more rectangles and make another spiral in the same manner. Repeat this until all spirals are laid out. Now, take a handsaw and carefully saw on the spiraled layout line to a depth of the desired spiral, **Figure 11-10**.

Using a carving chisel or a fluting chisel, begin to cut the spirals around the object, keeping your cut on either the right, **Figure 11-11**, or on

Figure 11-8. Draw parallel lines horizontally along the piece to be fluted.

Figure 11-9. Draw a number of equally spaced lines around the spindle, then draw diagonal lines to create the spiral line.

Figure 11-10. Use a hand saw to make a groove on the spiral line. This groove will serve as a guide for the chisel as the spiral groove is cut.

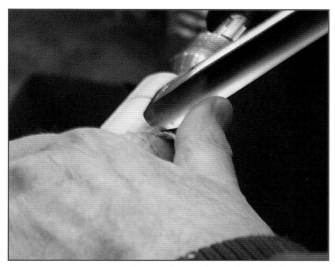

Figure 11-11. Carve along the right edge of the saw cut. This is the beginning of the spiral flute.

Figure 11-12. Use the chisel to cut on the left edge of the saw cut, creating the basic flute shape.

the left side of the saw cut, **Figure 11-12**. Rotate the lathe by hand as you make the cut and the chisel will follow the line of the spiral quite readily. Cut the spiral groove to the desired depth and then use round files, **Figure 11-13**, and a round dowel with sandpaper wrapped around it to finish up the spiral grooves. When finished the double spiral should look something like the one in **Figure 11-14**.

If one is doing spiraling on a hollow form, it may be desirable to make your saw cut all of the way through the wall of the vessel. The final spiraled vessel will then have open spiraled pieces that must be shaped for best effect, as shown in **Figure 3-1** on page 34.

If cutting flutes, only the equally spaced parallel lines need to be drawn and the chisel is then guided along each line using the tool rest as a guide. It is best to use a chisel with the flute shape closest to the desired flute.

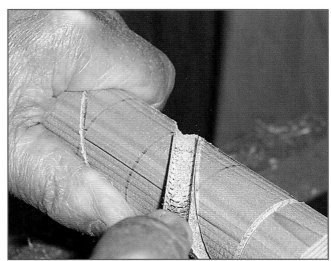

Figure 11-13. A rasp further refines the flutes.

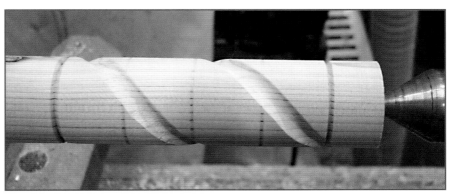

Figure 11-14. This is the finished spiral.

Q How can I cut spirals and flutes with a router?

Using a router to cut flutes and spirals requires a structure that sets over the lathe bed and holds the router, **Figure 11-15**. The router moves along the axis of rotation of the lathe, and the router bit cuts a groove, **Figure 11-16**. This fixture can be used easily to rout flutes in a straight spindle. It does not work well over the curved surfaces of a spindle. To cut spirals, it is necessary to rig up a cable and pulley arrangement that is connected to the lathe spindle in such a way that as the lathe spindle is rotated by hand, the router is pulled along it to cut the spiral line. This technique is not worth spending the time to set up, unless a large number of spiraled spindles are needed. Legacy Ornamental Mills produces a machine for this type of work, **Figure 11-17**.

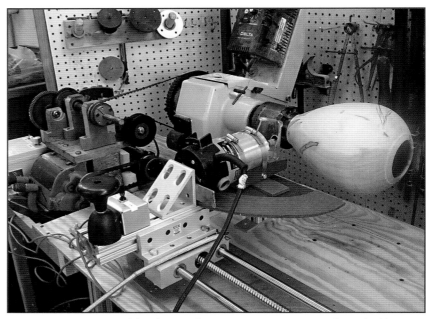

Figure 11-15. Jim Kohlenberger's set-up can cut spirals in hollow vessels. The router moves in concert with the rotating workpiece.

Figure 11-16. After routing, Kohlenberger can carve and sand the flutes.

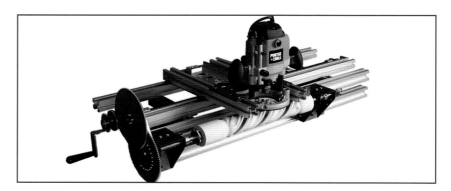

Figure 11-17. The Legacy Revo Craft Master routs flutes in turned cylinders. The crank rotates the spindle and moves the router.

Q How can I use pyrography to enhance my turnings?

Pyrography is wood burning and there are some excellent wood-burning tools on the market to use in decorating or enhancing a bland piece of wood. These techniques are used in some cases to simply highlight some feature such as a groove or circle on the rim of a platter. They are also used to create extensive effects such as David Nittman's basket illusion pieces, **Figure 11-18**. Since pyrography is simply burning, it is not always done with a wood burning machine, but with other simpler and less costly methods.

Figure 11-18. David Nittman, basket illusion in turned and carved wood.

Q Tell me about these less costly methods of doing pyrography?

One of the most common methods of enhancing a turned object with burning is to make burned grooves. A couple of burned grooves can add considerably to the looks of a piece of bland wood. These are generally done with some method that will create enough heat to char the wood in the groove. With this technique, a groove is first cut in the wood and then the object creating the heat is brought in contact with the rotating wood. The heat generated will char the wood and produce a nice effect. On pieces turned in the spindle mode, for example, a wire is generally used to create the heat and char the wood. It is a good idea to attach handles to each end of the wire, to avoid burning your hands. **Figure 11-19** shows a wire being used to burn a groove in a spindle.

When you want to burn a groove in a platter, a wire cannot be used, but you can use very stiff sandpaper on edge to char the groove.

Figure 11-19. Use a wire to burn a ring on a spindle.

These methods simply generate heat between the rotating wood and some material brought in contact with it. Higher speeds are required for best effect. Any blunt object can be used to good effect, including another piece of wood.

Q What about using a wood-burning machine?

Figure 11-20. Molly Winton textured this piece by burning the wood.

There are two ways in which these machines are used. One method is to use fine tips to make lines and do artwork on the wood. You can also use shaped brands made from wire, or copper nails that have had their heads filed, to make specific shapes.

Molly Winton, a local woodturning artist, uses both techniques to good effect in her turned and burned hollow forms. Molly, and a number of other local artists, have been introduced to pyrography by Graeme Priddle of New Zealand, who uses pyrography extensively in his work. **Figure 11-20** shows one of Molly's turned and burned pieces.

Q How about adding color to my work?

Figure 11-21. Jimmy Clewes completed the coloring of this piece before removing it from the lathe.

Color is normally added to work because the wood is so bland that it needs something to give it life; however, it may also be added to enhance the grain of nicely figured woods. In this latter case the color should be more of a translucent stain rather than an opaque color. Jimmy Clewes of England commonly uses alcohol-based colors on his platter rims. These colors highlight the rim but do not entirely hide the grain of the platter. He applies the color to the rim before he hollows the platter, so that he gets a clean definition between the rim and the rest of the platter. **Figure 11-21** shows one of Jimmy Clewes' platters before it was removed from the lathe.

The application of color to any turned object should be done with an artistic eye rather than simply dabbing on color to supposedly enhance the piece. When done with an artist's eye, the addition of color can be quite striking.

Q How can I decorate my work with inlays?

There are many ways to add inlays to a turning, but the simplest is to drill holes in the rim and glue in a contrasting wood dowel. In **Figure 11-22**, I am using the Oneway drilling fixture to hold the drill in the same position while drilling the holes around the rim of the bowl. This fixture enables you to set the angle and the depth of drilling. I drilled a hole at each of the 24 indexing positions on my lathe. I glued a side-grain dowel, cut from a board with a plug cutter, into each hole. When the glue had set I cut the plugs away and sanded the surface smooth. The finished bowl rim is shown in **Figure 11-23**.

There are two other illustrations worth looking at for more ideas on decorating. Both were made by Hawaiian woodturners. **Figure 11-24** shows a bowl turned by Cliff Johns, who used a texturing pattern on its rim. **Figure 11-25** is a bowl turned and decorated by Sharon Doughtie, who uses Keltic designs in virtually all of her work. The surface of this bowl was textured and painted or stained black, with the design left in natural wood color, except for the red dots. What the many pieces shown in this chapter illustrate is that what you do to enhance appearance depends largely upon your artistic ability and your imagination.

Figure 11-22. The Oneway drilling fixture helps drill 24 indexed holes in the rim of the bowl.

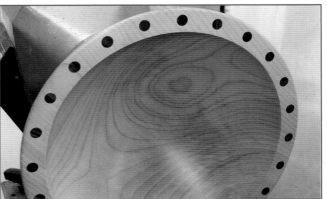

Figure 11-23. The contrasting color dowels have been glued in and turned off.

Figure 11-24. Bowl by Cliff Johns of Hawaii.

Figure 11-25. Decorated bowl by Sharon Doughtie.

FAQ 12

Finishing

Q How do I finish my turnings?

Finishing is special to the turner. Each of us develops our own particular finish. In the process of arriving at your finish, you may try nearly every commercially available finish. What works best for you may not work at all for others.

I wish I could give you the magic answer, but I can only give you some ideas based on the finishes that I've used and what the results have been for me.

The finishing of a turned piece involves two stages: first, smoothing the work by scraping, sanding, or burnishing; and second, sealing the smoothed surface with a mixture containing oil or varnish or both.

Wally Dickerman, who has been turning wood for 60 years, produces beautiful, thin-walled vessels that simply shine. Wally says the shine must be put on before the finish is applied. He sands up to 1200-grit or finer. Then he applies his finish. Wally may spend an entire day finishing a piece. Wally does what many others do not do, he makes the wood as smooth as he possibly can before beginning to finish. Wally finishes by sanding really smooth, and then seals in the finish.

Personally, I'm lazy. I belong to the "I hate to sand club. For a long time, I started with about 100-grit or 120-grit paper and sanded down to 220-grit or 240-grit and then quit. I rubbed on some oil and let it go at that, and sometimes applied some wax over the oil. This finish never did shine.

Q How do I smooth my piece before applying finish?

Many prominent turners don't "make it smooth" when they finish a turning. They are sand-blasting, stippling, or grooving. However, most average turners do make their work as smooth as they can, and so should you, before you move on to any of those enhancements described in Chapter 11. Sand with progressively finer sandpaper up to 240-grit or even to 600-grit, followed by a little burnishing with a handful of shavings.

In his book *Turning Wood*, Richard Raffan says that for turnings intended for use, 240-grit is fine enough. Turners who make a living from their work do not sand much below 240-grit. It takes too long.

You can sand quickly using a rotary sander mounted in a drill motor, with replaceable disks. I use a 2-inch hook and loop type of disk. I keep disks on hand from about 60-grit to 600-grit. I also use Klingspor's 1 inch disk on the inside of small bowls; it also is handy for cleaning up the foot of a bowl. I also have a self-powered rotary sander, as shown on page 20. Rotary sanders are faster than hand-held sandpaper and less likely to leave scratches.

Maybe you don't want to buy a rotary sander. You would rather use flat sandpaper. OK, cut the paper into strips 2-1/2 inches to 3 inches (60mm to 75mm) wide and fold the strips into thirds. To protect your fingers from frictional heat, use a piece of foam rubber about 2 inches (50mm) square as a backer. This keeps the heat away and, I believe, does a better job on the surface too. Some turners prefer a thin piece of soft leather.

Ok, let's start sanding.

Start with the finest grit that will smooth the surface of the turning. Sometimes you can't get out all of the flaws with that grit, so you go back to a coarser grit. If the wood has been exceptionally stubborn and the turned surface is not level, then the sandpaper needs to be coarse, 80-grit, 60-grit, or even 40-grit. You can do a lot of shaping with 40-grit sandpaper, but you can also create some really deep scratches.

If I can't quickly sand clean with 100-grit paper, I figure that I need to go back to the turning tools.

When turning with a skew, I start sanding with 240-grit paper. The surface left by a skew might best be burnished with a handful of shavings and left as is.

Sand until the surface is as smooth as that grit is likely to make it, and until all of the scratches made by a coarser grit have been removed. Then, move to the next finer grit. By folding the sandpaper in thirds, you have three fresh surfaces to work with. I start with 100-grit or 150-grit, move to 180-grit, then 220-grit or 240-grit, then 320-grit and finally to 400-grit. Exotic woods such as ironwood, lignum vitae, redheart, ziricote, and cocobolo can generally be started with 240-grit and go to 600-grit.

It doesn't matter whether you use hand-held sandpaper or a rotary sander, the grit sequence should be the same. Fine steel wool, or a handful of fine shavings held against the rotating surface, will burnish an already smooth surface to make it shine. The better the shine from sanding and polishing, the better the finished piece will look.

Q How do I seal the surface?

Every turner likes something different to seal the wood. Some prefer a simple oil finish, allowed to soak in, wiped off, and burnished with a rag. The variations are in the oil and you should try all the nontoxic oils to find the one that works best for you. Some, such as tung oil, contain hardeners, varnishes, and dryers.

You can have a shiny surface if your wood was shiny before you applied the oil. If the oil raises the grain of the wood, cut it back with 400-grit or 600-grit wet/dry sandpaper dipped in oil.

Some production turners have a tub of mineral oil, and they just soak the piece half an hour before wiping and lightly buffing.

Q What finishes are safe for food utensils?

A salad bowl shouldn't shine. It should be treated with an oil that occasionally can be reapplied to renew the finish. Some turners recommend mineral oil. Others recommend cooking oils such as olive oil, or peanut oil. Some use linseed oil, or Danish oil. I use walnut oil on kitchen items. I've also used a commercial mixture of nut oils, called Preserve, which dries quickly. Walnut oil is less expensive but does not dry as quickly.

I simply flood the surface and rub it in as much as possible. I let it soak for a while and then wipe off the oil and buff it with a soft cloth.

I also use this finish on children's toys. The oil brings the wood to life and is nontoxic in case the toy goes into the mouth. Toys don't need a gloss finish, because they are going to be used and abused. A gloss finish would look tatty in a very short time.

Any oil finish will need to be refreshed occasionally, so you should advise your customer or recipient accordingly.

Q What about wax finishes?

I use beeswax finishes on spinner tops and little end-grain boxes. I also use beeswax to lubricate wood threads. There are two that I especially like, Kerf's Wood Creme and Clapham's Salad Bowl Finish.

Kerf's Wood Creme is formulated for cutting boards and culinary utensils, or any item that may contact food or the mouths of people or animals. It's made from food-grade ingredients and will never turn rancid. It can be used over oil-based finishes or directly on bare wood.

The folks who make Clapham's are full-time beekeepers who came up with products to use their excess beeswax. Their salad bowl finish was formulated for salad and fruit bowls, butcher blocks, and cutting boards. It is edible.

Q What is French polish?

In one of her videos Bonnie Klein tells how to make a French polish mixture. I use it on bottle stoppers and small bowls. I haven't had real good luck using it on larger bowls.

This finish is made up of equal parts shellac, alcohol, and boiled linseed oil. Shake the bottle, then apply enough to soak into the wood. With the lathe running, buff in the finish using the wet part of the rag. Shift to a dry part of the rag and buff dry. Use 400-grit or 600-grit wet/dry sandpaper, or 0000 steel wool, to remove any whiskers. Then apply the wet area of the rag again to give the piece its final polish.

The higher the polish of the wood before applying the polish, the higher the gloss after.

I read about a turner who sands his work to a high gloss and floods the surface with Red Label Hot Stuff cyanoacrylate glue. He allows the glue to set naturally, no accelerator, and sands with 400-grit or 600 grit or finer. Then, he applies the French polish to obtain a super high-gloss finish that is impervious to water, alcohol, and other chemicals.

Cyanoacrylate can glue your fingers together, or to the workpiece, or the lathe. Keep the glue solvent handy.

Q What about spray-on finishes?

I don't personally care for painted or sprayed finishes, although I do occasionally use them. I've used Deft and Durathane. The spray type works better for me than the brushing type. I apply a light coat, and sand with 600-grit sandpaper and 0000 steel wool the following day. Then another coat and repeat the sanding. I do this for four or five applications over a week's time, and leave the last coat as sprayed. This makes a very shiny bowl that looks like it has been dipped in clear plastic.

Q Can you buff to get a shine?

Buffing is one way to take that oiled surface to an ultra shine. Many people use different methods of buffing; I like the Beall system. It consists of three buffing wheels, two abrasives (tripoli and white diamond), carnauba wax, and a quick-change attachment for the shaft of an electric motor. You can also get a Morse taper adapter.

You begin by sanding to 220-grit, then apply a coat of a drying oil such as Watco. When the oil is completely dry, buff first with the tripoli, follow with white diamond, and finally, buff on the hard carnauba wax. Be sure to change wheels for each compound. It takes only a few minutes and leaves a nice soft-gloss finish.

One caution: When buffing, hold tight to the workpiece because the buffing wheel can grab and throw it across the room.

Appendix A Recommended List of Woodturning Books

This is a short list of books on woodturning. I own, and have read, a great many more than are listed here. Out of that many, I have selected a few titles for inclusion here that I feel are a must read for particular topics. My guides when I started turning were the books and videos by Richard Raffan. As a result, all of Richard Raffan's books are highly recommended. The following list is divided into areas of woodturning expertise:

Books of general interest to woodturners

A Guide to Work-Holding on the Lathe, by Fred Holder

Turning Wood with Richard Raffan, by Richard Raffan

Turning Projects with Richard Raffan, by Richard Raffan

Turning Bowls, by Richard Raffan

Turning Boxes, by Richard Raffan

Woodturning: A Foundation Course, by Keith Rowley

Woodturning Projects: A Workshop Guide to Shapes, by Mark Baker

Classic Woodturning Projects with Bonnie Klein: 12 Skill-building Designs, by Bonnie Klein

Woodturning Techniques, by Mike Darlow

Woodturning Methods, by Mike Darlow

The Fundamentals of Woodturning, by Mike Darlow

The Practice of Woodturning, by Mike Darlow

Woodturning Design (Mike Darlow's Woodturning Series, Number 4), by Mike Darlow

Specialty books

Making Screw Threads in Wood, by Fred Holder

Techniques of Spiral Work, by Stewart Mortimer

The Art of Segmented Woodturning, by Malcolm Tibbetts

Turning Pens and Pencils, by Rex Burningham & Kip Christensen

Segmented Woodturning, by William Smith

Woodturning Wizardry, by David Springett

Selling your work

Make Money from Woodturning, by Ann and Bob Phillips

Appendix **B** List of Woodturning Magazines

There are only a few magazines devoted exclusively to the topic of woodturning. They are listed below:

American Woodturner, published quarterly by the American Association of Woodturners, 222 Landmark Center, 75 W. Fifth Street, St. Paul, MN 55102-1431 USA. The editor is Carl Voss. The web site is: www.woodturner.org. This is an excellent magazine that is published four times each year and mailed to members of the association. Membership is $40 inside the United States, $45 in Canada, and $65 overseas.

More Woodturning, published ten times each year: monthly except for April and October, Post Office Box 2168, Snohomish, Washington 98291 USA. The editor and publisher is Fred Holder. The web site is www.fholder.com/Woodturning/woodturn.htm. It is available as a print subscription with a color cover or as an Internet subscription with the magazine in PDF format and in full color. The magazine is available for $32 per year inside the United States, $39.50 for Canada, and $42 overseas. Canada and overseas locations do not have to pay extra for the PDF version which is distributed from the web site.

Woodturning, published every four weeks by the Guild of Master Craftsman Publications Ltd., 166 High Street, Lewes, East Sussex BN7 1XU, England. The editor is Colin Simpson. This is an excellent magazine, which is published 13 times each year in full color. The magazine is available in the United States for $82.80 per year.

Woodturning Design, published quarterly by All American Crafts, Inc., 7 Waterloo Road, Stanhope, NJ 07874. Telephone: 800-940-6591. The editor is Joseph M. Herrmann. This is one of the newest woodturning magazines on the market. It is printed in full color and is an excellent project book. The web site is www.woodturningdesign.com. The subscription price is $19.97 for four issues per year.

Appendix C Woods for Turning

It should be noted that virtually any wood may be turned. However, this list covers those woods that have been found the most suitable.

Q What are some of the softwoods that may be turned with sharp tools?

Bass Wood
Butternut
Cedar
Douglas Fir
White Pine

Q What are some of the harder and more common woods that are normally turned?

Alder
Apple
Ash
Beech
Birch
Box Elder (also a Maple)
Citrus woods (Orange, Lime, Lemon, Grapefruit)
Cherry
Chestnut
Cottonwood
Elm
Hickory
Holly
Horse Chestnut
Laburnum
Locust
Mahogany
Maple:
  Big Leaf Maple
  Rock or Hard Maple
Oak
Osage Orange
Peach
Pear
Plum
Rosewood
Tulipwood

Walnut:
  American Black Walnut
  English Walnut
Willow
Yew
Zebrawood

Q What are some of the extremely hard and dense woods that will hold a hand chased thread?

African Blackwood
Boxwood
Cocobolo
Lignum-vitae

Appendix D Woodturning Terms

This appendix is a compilation of woodturning terms that the reader may encounter in this book or in their reading in woodturning magazines.

Axis of rotation of the lathe:
This is an imaginary point at the exact center of the rotation of the headstock spindle. This may be represented by an imaginary line that runs between a drive center mounted in the headstock spindle and a center mounted in the tailstock spindle.

Banjo:
The part of the tool rest assembly that is bolted to the bed of the lathe.

Bed of lathe:
The main structure of the lathe, which is bolted to the stand. The machined surface on which the headstock assembly, the tool rest assembly, and the tailstock assembly are attached is called the ways of the lathe bed. In some cases the headstock assembly is mounted in a casting that is a part of the lathe bed.

Blank (turning blank):
Refers to the piece of wood that has been prepared for mounting on the lathe for turning. In the case of blanks for spindle turning, the grain runs along the length of the blank so that the grain is parallel to the axis of rotation of the lathe. This is also the case for hollow forms in general. The blank for a bowl or platter will have the grain running across the blank so that when mounted on the lathe the grain will be perpendicular to the axis of rotation.

Chatterwork:
This is a pattern that is created when either the wood or the tool flexes as the wood is cut. It may be created with a very flexible cutting tool that will vibrate when it is applied to the wood. This type of created chatterwork, is best done on end grain surfaces.

Checking:
These are small cracks that develop in the end of wood as it dries. They do not generally go very deep and are the main reason for leaving a half log about two inches longer than it is wide when being saved as a bowl blank.

Crotch wood:
This is wood in the junction area where a tree has branched out in two directions. The wood in these areas is generally highly figured and can produce a beautiful turning.

Flutes:
These are equally spaced grooves around a spindle or other form of turning. They may be cut by some machining method or cut by hand with a wood chisel or gouge.

Gouge:
A turning tool of U shape cross section that is used for cutting on both spindle and faceplate turning.

Grain:
These are the fibers of the wood that extend from the base of the tree to the very top most portion. The finer and closer together these fibers grow, the harder and denser the wood. For a simplified example, a bundle of straws is a close approximation to the grain structure of a piece of wood.

Hardwood:
Hardwood is normally considered to come from trees or shrubs, which lose their leaves in the winter. This wood may be very soft and stringy, such as willow, or very dense and hard such as boxwood.

Heartwood:
The heartwood of the tree is that part which is no longer growing. It is generally the darkest in color and the hardest part of the tree.

Natural edge:
This refers to a bowl or vase wherein the outside of the tree (or the bark) is a part of the rim of the vessel. In the case of a bowl, the base is toward the center of the tree and the top is of the shape generated by the outside of the tree.

Live center:
A live center, as referred to in this book, is a tailstock center in which a bearing assembly allows the center point to rotate while the tang mounted in the tailstock spindle does not rotate. In the early days of woodturning, the term live center referred to the drive center in the headstock spindle.

Power sanding:
This term refers to the use of a drill motor or other devise to rotate a disk on which sandpaper has been mounted.

Rough turning:
This refers to the turning of an object to general shape, but leaving it oversize to allow the wood to move as it changes its moisture content to stabilize with its current environment. Even when the wood is supposedly completely dry, it is a good idea to rough turn pieces such as little boxes and allow them to further dry for a few days before final turning to size and final fitting of the lids.

Sapwood:
That portion of the tree which was still alive and growing when it was harvested. The sapwood is generally much lighter in color than the heartwood and may also be softer than the heartwood.

Scraper:
A tool, rectangular in cross section, that is ground with a fairly steep bevel. The actual cutting edge is the little burr turned up on the edge of the tool when it is sharpened. The tool is used with the handle elevated to bring the cutting edge of the burr into contact with the wood. The cut is normally made at the center line of the rotating wood.

Skew chisel:
This is a tool, rectangular in cross section, with the cutting edge skewed at about 70 degrees to the length of the tool. The cutting edge is on the center line of the thickness of the tool; i.e., the tool has a double bevel angle that puts the cutting edge at the center of the thickness of the tool.

Spindle:
On each lathe there are at least two spindles: the headstock spindle, or drive spindle, and the tailstock spindle. The headstock spindle rotates and provides the drive for the wood. The tailstock spindle does not rotate, but moves in and out to allow for adjustment of tension on a piece of wood held between centers.

Seasoning:
Allowing wood to dry and declare itself. When seasoning wood, it is good to stack it with stickers between each layer to allow air to flow to all sides of the wood. This is especially true when the wood has been sawn into planks.

Shear scraping:
A method of scraping in which the tool's cutting edge is rotated approximately 45 degrees from the horizontal, which allows the cutting edge to slice the wood rather than scrape it.

Softwood:
Generally woods that are evergreen, i.e., do not lose their leaves or needles in the winter.

Stickers:
Thin strips of wood used to separate wet wood when it is stacked for drying. They will vary in thickness from 1/4" to 3/4", the latter being my preference for most wood drying.

Spalted wood:
Spalted wood is wood that has been attacked by fungi that leave black lines and patterns in the wood. This is the first stage of rotting and wood that has been spalted for too long is generally quite difficult to turn.

Spiral flutes:
Grooves that spiral around the surface of a turned object. The flutes are generally equally spaced apart and are laid out to spiral one or more full turns over the length of the spiral. They may be cut by machine or by hand with a carving chisel or gouge.

Tailstock:
The assembly mounted on the bed of the lathe that is furthest from the headstock. Its purpose it to provide support for wood between its center point and the center point on the headstock spindle. When wood is mounted on a faceplate, the tailstock may be removed from the lathe to allow more room to work.

Tool rest:
The platform on which turning tools are rested before they are applied to the rotating wood. The normal height for the tool rest puts the cutting edge of the tool at near center of rotation of the wood to be turned.

Tear out:
Small pieces of wood grain that are pulled out of the wood surface instead of being cleanly cut by the slicing of the turning tool. This is most common on those portions of a bowl's surface which contains end grain.

Ways:
The machined surface on the bed of the lathe to which the headstock, tool rest assembly, and the tailstock are mounted. This generally has a machined space down its center dividing the surface into two parts so that the attached assemblies are centered horizontally in alignment with the axis of rotation of the lathe.

Wet turning:
Turning freshly cut wood which contains a great deal of water. It is normal in wet turning to turn the wood, say a bowl, to shape but leaving the wall thickness about 10 percent of the diameter of the bowl. It is, however, possible to wet turn a bowl or vessel to final size and wall thickness, sand it wet, apply finish and then allow it to declare itself. In the case of natural edge bowls, this can often be very effective since the bowl will actually become oval.

Appendix E What You Need to Get Started

What you need to get started in woodturning depends on what you want to make. Regardless of what you plan to turn, you will need the following items as a minimum, along with a place to set up and work:

1. A lathe;

2. A chuck to hold the work on the lathe;

3. A grinder to sharpen your turning tools;

4. A saw to cut up wood (preferably a bandsaw or an electric chainsaw);

5. Turning tools;

6. Measuring tools;

7. Wood.

If you wish to try your hand at turning smaller items, such as pens, bottle stoppers, and goblets, the following recommendations would apply:

Lathe

One of the small lathes listed in Table I. The best and most expensive of these lathes is the Vicmarc VL-100, an expenditure of $400 to $750 depending on which power unit you choose. A second recommendation would be the Jet Mini Lathe with a price from $300 to $380, depending on the power unit. There are, of course, a number of other lathes listed in Table I, any of which can serve as starter lathes. I have experience with, and can recommend, either of the two mentioned here.

Chuck

There are many good chucks on the market; however, if you are starting with a small lathe and trying to keep the cost down, I recommend the NOVA G3 chuck for use with your mini-lathe at a cost of about $145. A second choice would be the SuperNova2 at a cost of about $200. The Oneway Talon chuck or the Vicmarc 3-1/2 inch (90mm) chuck will run around $220.

Grinder

About the best buy on a grinder is the slow-speed 8-inch (200mm) grinder from Woodcraft Supply. It comes with white aluminum oxide wheels and will cost about $100. I also recommend a sharpening jig, because sharpening tools is a very challenging task for a beginner that is much simplified with a jig. There are two that I have experience with: the Oneway Wolverine sharpening system for about $150 and the Tru-Grind sharpening system also for about $150.

Saw to cut up wood

As a minimum one needs a chainsaw to cut wood blanks for turning. An electric chainsaw can be purchased for around $50 to $60. It will not, however, be nearly as handy or as versatile as a band saw. I recommend the Grizzly 14 inch (350mm) band saw, around $500. I used one for several years before I outgrew it.

Turning tools

You can buy an inexpensive set of high speed tools from Harbor Freight for under $100, but I really recommend purchasing single tools as you need them, rather than a set. I have found that any of the name-brand tool makers -- Robert Sorby, Henry Taylor, Ashley Iles, Hamlet, and Crown -- are all good. The prices will vary from manufacturer to manufacturer, but high-speed steel tools from any of these will serve you well. As a minimum, I recommend the following:

Spindle gouge, 3/8 inch (10mm) or 1/2 inch (12,5mm), about $30 to $35.

Skew chisel, 1/2 inch (12,5mm) and 3/4 inch (19 or 20mm), between $30 and $40 each.

Diamond parting tool, 3/16 inch (5mm), $40 to $45.

Roughing gouge, 3/4 inch (20mm), $45.

Bowl gouge, 3/8 inch (10mm) or 1/2 inch (12,5mm), $45 to $55.

Measuring Tools
I carry a 3-foot (900mm) steel tape in my pocket all of the time and highly recommend one, cost about $10 or less, plus a 6-inch (150mm) outside caliper, the spring style works great, for measuring wall thickness and to set diameters on spindles, about $10. An 8-inch (200mm) wing compass is also nice to have for laying out bowl blanks and drawing circles to use when cutting to size, about $25.

Wood
You can purchase prepared wood from suppliers like Woodcraft and Craft Supplies USA, or you can scrounge the neighborhood for free wood. Once people know you turn wood, free wood will come from out of nowhere because trees are always coming down and people hate to burn nice wood like fruit woods, nut woods, and maple.

Your total cost to start will run $1,000 to $1,500, depending upon which lathe you purchase and which brand of turning tools you select.

The next level of growth might be to something like the NOVA model 1624-44 lathe, which sells for about $1,000. This would then increase your investment to between $2,000 and $2,500, with a more expensive chuck and a more expensive lathe and perhaps a few more turning tools.

Woodturning is not an inexpensive hobby, but it can provide a lot of rewarding hours in the shop and some nice items to use as Christmas gifts or to sell at a local bazaar.

More great woodworking books from Linden Publishing

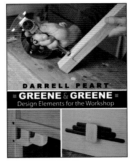
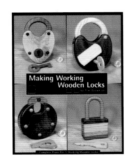
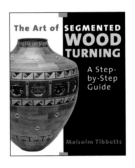
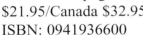
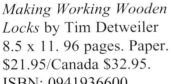
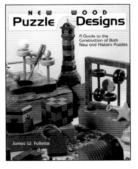

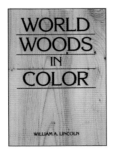